DATE DUE

			PRINTED IN U.S.A.

The End of the Draft

RANDOM HOUSE

New York

Prefaces by

SENATOR MARK O. HATFIELD &
SENATOR GEORGE McGOVERN

The End of the Draft

A proposal for abolishing conscription

and for a volunteer army,

for popular resistance to militarism

and the restoration of individual freedom

THOMAS REEVES
and KARL HESS

78927 ✓

Library of Congress Catalog Card Number: 78–117688

Manufactured in the United States of America by
The Colonial Press, Inc. Clinton, Massachusetts
9   8   7   6   5   4   3   2

FIRST EDITION

For GUNILLA and LIZ
and for
GREGG ROGERS,
whose death brought the war home

Acknowledgments

Tom Reeves and Karl Hess thank Stewart Kemp, economist for the Gates Commission, for his thorough research in chapter 8. Fielding McGehee has given many hours to research and rewriting. His persevering consultation, especially on foreign policy and military dissent, has been very helpful. Thanks are also due to Richard Cohen, Hally Montague, Josephine Lee Davis, Leigh Larsen, Katherine Lowndes Darby, Martha Adams, Linda Gubala, and Jim Hall.

The research was made possible by the National Council to Repeal the Draft, 101 D St., S.E., Washington, D.C. The Council takes no responsibility for content.

Prefaces

The draft has been with us for nearly thirty years, the first decade of which was in response to World War II and its immediate aftermath. The last two decades, however, mark the first time in our history that there has been peacetime conscription in America.

It is a poignant commentary on this country that until the late sixties, there was very little negative reaction to the draft from public officials, intellectuals, parents, or youth. Initiated by criticizing United States policy in Vietnam, anti-draft activity is now a self-sustaining effort—focusing on conscription's inherent inequities, injustices and inefficiencies—as well as focusing upon one aspect of a greater problem within our society: the military-industrial-political-educational complex. It is necessary to understand the draft from these two perspectives to fully grasp its iniquitous and debilitating effects on our country.

Having been through the stages of apathy-fear, problem

discernment and definition, and critical analysis, we are now at a fourth stage: constructive solution. Vietnam has been the instigator of this process of increasing concern and has led to the heightened examination of our government's policies and national priorities.

Karl Hess and Tom Reeves, with Stuart Kemp, have done an excellent job not only in stating the case against the draft but also in offering many suggestions as to how to regain our balance domestically and internationally. For, as they point out, merely abolishing peacetime conscription and establishing a volunteer military does not solve the problems we face: it is a key to the door, a first step.

They take us through the inequities inherent within the draft, set a philosophical framework, analyze the Orwellian document of the Selective Service System's memo on channeling, point to the contextual framework surrounding the draft, and propose steps which should be taken to re-establish and reorganize our national priorities in accordance with our Constitution and, a seemingly forgotten document, the Declaration of Independence.

It is interesting to note that while one may disagree with some, if not all, of the suggestions for change or for implementing change made by the authors, many of the proposals are already realities. For instance, non-violent obstructionist tactics and parallel institutions, such as those in education and in Congress (for example, Members of Congress for Peace through Law), are already developing and will continue to flourish until currently dysfunctional institutions are either revitalized, replaced, or abolished.

The problem of popular control of the government and its agencies is really the theme of this book. The authors firmly believe that the government and its extensions should be responsible and responsive to the people, not the reverse.

I commend this book to anyone interested in the issues

surrounding the draft and the revolution we face in our society today. The analysis of our country's current crisis is very perceptive, and while I may not agree with every one of the authors' suggestions for implementing change, the proposals they make and the attitude they present are representative of a much needed revitalized faith in the future of the United States, its institution, its leaders, and in ourselves.

Mark O. Hatfield

Any careful analysis of the draft, and there have been a number in recent years, leaves one wondering how it has managed to hang on so long. Its justifications smack far more of fable than of fact, and it is repugnant to nearly every shade of American political philosophy—from Barry Goldwater to George McGovern, and further at both ends.

A nation founded on human liberty and individual dignity, and peopled in good part by escapees from compulsion in other lands, should have a natural distaste for conscription. We have, in fact, decided once through the devastation of civil war that freedom and involuntary servitude cannot coexist. On principle, the draft is as foreign as anything can be to the ideals we profess as a free, libertarian society.

Thus, for most of our history we have rejected it unless our national survival itself has been at stake. It was first used sparingly during the Civil War and has never been employed, until the last two decades, except in cases of war duly declared by the Congress.

As had always been the case, the draft expired again after World War II. But the respite was brief. After a pervasive Pentagon campaign exploiting fear of the Soviet Union—our World War II ally turned Cold War adversary—the Congress in 1948 adopted the country's first peacetime draft. It has remained, even though the belief that gave it birth—that land war with Russia was imminent, leaving no time for mobilization—has long since grown stale and even incredible in an age of nuclear terror.

Surely the burden of proof for such an aberration must rest with those who demand it. Yet they have not been required to carry it. For most of the past twenty-two years Congress has been docile and receptive to simple assertions of the draft's necessity. But for Vietnam, a conflict whose wisdom is blatantly questionable and into which thousands of young Americans have been impelled against their will, that state of affairs might have continued.

The questioning has at last begun. And as the authors of this work make clear, the solution should not be far behind—if we can believe that our political system is responsive to rationality.

First we must pose the precise issue, and in this process the clear inadequacy of draft reform, as opposed to draft repeal, is exposed. If we accept the conclusion that the nation needs a military force of some size, and most of us do while differing sharply on numbers, our central problem is not in choosing who among us will serve. It is determining how enough manpower can be attracted. Whether the choice is based on pure chance or on the prejudices of someone in the vast Selective Service network, any draft system does the attracting by force. Any draft tells young men, willing or not, that they must serve or be jailed. It is that simple issue which must be faced by any plan that purports to improve the system, and it cannot be faced without repeal.

The President's Commission on an All-Volunteer Armed Force, led by former Defense Secretary Thomas S. Gates, reported early in 1970 that the draft can be ended now; that a voluntary force is feasible. What, then, prevents action?

Some fear the costs of attracting volunteers. They first neglect the intolerable intangible costs exacted by compulsory service in a free society. They neglect, too, that the draft does not mean escape from the economic costs of fair remuneration for military manpower; it merely shifts them to the young draftee who must not only serve against his will but must also pay the equivalent of a heavy tax for the privilege. But even more persuasively, the Gates Commission has concluded that the real costs of improving the conditions of military service to the point where enough volunteers would come forward would be far less than most of us would expect. Cost is clearly not a barrier, nor should it be.

Others have argued that an all-volunteer force will tend to create a special military ethos which will endanger civilian control of the military. But in truth the draft has little bearing on this subject. The individuals who control the military apparatus and make military decisions are already volunteers. Surely the responsibility for control of the military must be grasped by the President and by the Congress. We cannot expect much help from randomly selected forced laborers who rest at the bottom of the military hierarchy and who are taught to obey, without question, the commands of their superiors.

A related objection with much currency is that an all-volunteer force might more readily permit misconceived foreign ventures like Vietnam, or at least make them more difficult to end. But the draft did not prevent Vietnam, it has not ended it, and if we get into a similar war in the future, the draft would probably be reinstituted—placing us right back where we are today. As to prevention, I suspect that if anything, the voluntary force might serve as some restraint on Presidents and generals prone to military involvements, because they could not automatically count on forced manpower to do the fighting. Besides, this argument, like the one just mentioned, also expects more of the young draftee than we have a right to expect. It says to him, "We in the government, who are charged by the Constitution with direct responsibility over issues of war and peace, are afraid to exercise our wisdom. Therefore, we have devised a clever scheme. You go fight, take injuries, and be killed in a mistaken war. Then perhaps your parents and your friends will start objecting and others like you who have not yet been called will start protesting, and then they'll create a political climate in which we can act safely." Clearly we should seek other methods of inoculation against future Vietnams.

Karl Hess and Tom Reeves, whose joint authorship illustrates the breadth of today's opposition to the draft, supply in this book a careful analysis of these and other questions bearing on the role of military conscription in a free society. They will make converts.

They will also give advocates of draft repeal a new measure of confidence in the validity and the urgency of their cause, in turn moving us closer to the day when this monstrous system will finally be ended.

George McGovern

Contents

PREFACES: Senator Mark O. Hatfield and Senator
   George McGovern   *i x*

1. Youth versus the Violence Experts   *3*
2. The State and Its Citizens   *2 1*
3. The Kidnapped Dream   *2 8*
4. The Conscripted Mind   *4 5*
5. The Impacted Group   *6 6*
6. The Course of Control   *8 0*
7. The Draft and Public Policy   *9 1*
8. The Cost of Voluntary Defense   *1 0 3*
9. Military, Civilian, or Popular Control   *1 2 1*
10. After the Draft Is Ended   *1 5 3*

APPENDIX: Channeling   *1 9 3*

The End of the Draft

Chapter 1

Youth versus
the Violence Experts

Americans have usually thought of themselves as among the freest of men. Yet black Americans have never been free, and today many of our institutions are steadily and increasingly encroaching on the freedoms of the rest of us. Justice William O. Douglas speaks of the deterioration in the "freedom to be left alone."

These are the rights that distinguish us from all totalitarian regimes. The real enemies of freedom are not confined to any nation or any country. They are everywhere. They flourish where injustice, discrimination, ignorance, superstition, intolerance and arbitrary power exist. We cannot afford to inveigh against them abroad, unless we are alert to guard against them at home. Yet in recent years as we have denounced the loss of liberty abroad we have witnessed its decline here. We have indeed, been retreating from our democratic ideals at home. We have compromised them for security.[1]

In large part it is the presence of a huge "defense" establishment which threatens our freedom to be left alone. Once Americans had accepted the premise that the nation is under a severe threat of foreign domination in an age of total weaponry and escalating technology, the justification for nullifying many freedoms was established. Every modern "national security state" in a state of constant preparedness must involve a form of pragmatic socialism which means *state control*. By selling the otherwise watchful conservatives the myth of anticommunism, the liberals effectively muzzled the only likely opponents of any consequence to the steady growth of a centralized and allpowerful federal bureaucracy. It is important to remember that, even so, the loudest voices raised in warning were those of men like Robert A. Taft. Speaking of universal military training as "the most serious limitation on freedom that can be imagined," he said:

> It is useless to destroy totalitarianism in Germany and Japan and then establish it in the United States. . . . Government controls such as peacetime military conscription, which would have been indignantly rejected in the nineteenth century, are given serious consideration, even in this country. . . . Many people who indignantly deny any soft feeling for state control are advocates of measures which lead inevitably in that direction because they are dissatisfied with the necessarily slow progress involved in a government where all the people are given a voice. . . . The war has required a suspension of many freedoms, and the people have become so used to regulations that they almost forget what freedom is. The danger of totalitarian government is that the people do get used to it, as to a narcotic." [2]

A few, like Felix Morley, President of Haverford, saw measures like the draft as dangerous *primarily* because they threatened "to undermine the entire federal system of checks and balances" upon too much centralized power.[3] It was Eisenhower rather than Truman or Kennedy who gave the sober warning about a growing military-industrial complex. Any modern state, and particularly any which seeks to control the "rugged individualism" of the rich to protect the poor, must grow in scope and power. But that power may be balanced geographically or within the government system. There may be still a place—extended to most of the population—for the citizen to be left alone if he leaves others alone; to be free of control if he seeks to control no one. But a modern state that must be always prepared for war *cannot* leave anyone alone, for anyone left alone is a potential threat to national security.

The draft as an issue connected with the war and with the growth of the new style of military provides a case study of the problems of effectively opposing the groups which share the power based on violence. Its impact on our society shows at once its intimate tie with the antidemocratic trends present today. Representing an acceptance, in peacetime, of wartime measures it symbolizes the carryover of state emergency powers of all kinds. It helps to maintain the atmosphere and the myth of a nation in grave danger of attack by a foreign power. As an institution which holds power over life and death, it adds to the reservoir of precedents for the accepted powers of the state over its citizens.

The break with American tradition which the draft represents concerns conservatives, liberals and radicals. A coalition including Barry Goldwater and the Young Americans for Freedom, as well as George McGovern and the Vietnam Moratorium Committee, has joined to attack the draft. It is indicative of the difficulty of a clear opposition militarism that this coalition immediately evokes suspicion in some quarters that the primary concerns are not the evils of the draft but the possible ulterior motives. There is however no time to waste by limiting strategy to rhetoric or to safe allies. It is time to affirm the feasibility of freedom by ending the draft as a step toward protecting democratic institutions from military domination.

Our aim in this book is to find allies for freedom from every constituency—the left and the right, students and the military—where there is frustration instead of the former high hopes for liberty. In government some are deeply troubled by the shift to a military emphasis in almost every sector. Their commitment to the goals of a free and economically healthy society have been crushed by the demands of "national security." In the military some deplore the cheapening of a valuable service by a resort to the methods of slavery, and there are still others who fear the awesome growth of the military and the influence of the civilian managers from the Pentagon and elsewhere. To reach these people, we hope to expose the true significance of the draft in the context of an aggressive warfare bureaucracy.*

Setting aside the question of whether the United States is in real danger of external attack, the question that has been neglected to our peril concerns the effect of the defense preparations on the nation. The draft is intimately connected with that effect and its elimination would provide

---

* The welfare bureaucracy is thoroughly dependent on the warfare state, and is secondary to the needs of "national security." Because there has never been a firm resolution to put primary emphasis on the common good, measures like those in the War on Poverty have always been not only failures, but smokescreens to hide the real problems. The fact that the government is unresponsive to these basic needs shows that it is based on the interests of those in power whose own common good depends not on the good of all citizens, but on a successful hoax perpetrated against them.

an opening for change, for popular control, for a return to some degree of national health.

It is most important to realize that freedom from the draft is not only urgent but politically possible and that through it other freedoms will emerge. Change is coming in America. Everyone demands it, from the angry youth to the angry Agnew. Change is imminent because two powerful countertrends are crossing one another, and the draft is one point of confrontation. On the one hand we have the trend of a full-blown warfare state. The demands of that state have brought increased repression and polarization. One of the manifestations has been blitzkrieg attacks on institutions like draft boards, banks and chemical corporations. More and more a handful of self-appointed (or corporation-appointed) men control a centralizing but disintegrating society, and the realization of Machiavelli's dream appears: an all-powerful civilian state where military ends are absolute.*

The other trend is a hopeful one. There is something new about the protest by young people. As it coincides with a new awareness of the minorities and a growing dissatisfaction of part of the majority, it is taking both new substance and new force. This revolution, or "movement," or "youth phenomenon" has frightened adult America as nothing else aside from the black revolt, and the two are linked both in the history of the civil rights movement and in the mind of "middle America." The conspiracy trial of the Chicago Seven and reactions to it are the signs of the division in the nation over this phenomenon, and the extent of the shock and fear it has produced. There are some signs that the initial simplistic reactions of most Americans will not be sufficient to explain it away, and that it is having an impact

---

* See chapter 9.

on the entire society. Even the media, with their gift for packaging everything in pretty boxes that rob it of meaning, have failed to ruin it. As soon as one aspect of it seems co-opted, the revolution reasserts itself with new life. One of the jurors of the Chicago Seven voted with the others for conviction on some counts, but found her own life and understanding profoundly changed by Abbie Hoffman and the rest.

This youth "revolution," reaching far beyond the young, is intimately connected to the draft. The draft has not been a cause, or even a central stimulant of it, but the resistance to the draft has been a feature of its development, a hallmark of its style. An end to the draft will come, if at all, largely because of the revolting youth and because of the fear which the power groups have of them. An end of the draft will equally be an important step in the revolution's further political development from a creator of pressure on parents and politicians to an instrument for new forms of power to serve new sets of interests.

The right to draft derives from the most basic political dictum in the age which is just ending: the age of the nation-state. It is a principle which could accommodate equality, but never liberty. The draft makes the logical and absolute demand of the nation-state: that each citizen surrender even his life to the state, suspend his ethics and his beliefs before it, and serve it as his highest loyalty. The nation-state has, of course, not always been the key building block of politics. It has existed since some time between the Peace of Calais and the Peace of Westphalia. In 1648 Catholic and Lutheran princes declared an end to holy (ideological) wars. The artificial boundaries of their princedoms thereafter had only to withstand the test of geographical viability. Lesser or greater interest groups, religions, or other matters formerly of concern across the national boundaries remained within them. For all international political purposes, God was neither One nor Living anymore, nor were any beliefs beyond faith in the Prince.

Thus ended an age of universal strivings for one faith and one world, and began a far more practical set of national experiments of economic and political maturation "in one country," to paraphrase Stalin in Russia (where things developed late and hastily). In just over a century, most of the new nations were ready for the take-off into industrialism and for a bit of the dangerous game that has since been referred to as "democracy" or "republicanism." By the time of Napoleon I, all was ready for a modern state to thrive and flourish—within those appropriate geographical boundaries, but theoretically limited by no other bounds. The egalitarianism of Locke began to lose its freedom taint and the flurries of communism that prematurely occurred in the first flush season among such groups as Diggers and Levelers began to die down. In place of freedom sat the pragmatic wisdom of utility: the best for the most, all for one. It was the time also for conscription. If the state is seen as the result of a contract by all, then all must serve its needs in order to be served. There is equality in obedience to the whole (to Rousseau that meant the Universe, the Nation). There is equality in conscription, but also tyranny.

Before Napoleon conscription had been tried sporadically and had failed miserably. "Democracy" was a prerequisite for a successful draft. Here and there men had been impressed into service, but without the necessary legal basis for its widespread use or effectiveness—and most often they promptly ran away or demoralized the foreign mercenaries and other professionals. Those mercenaries worked by and large quite well for the enlightened despots who were enlightened because their despotism did not reach far enough to demand much obedience, but despotic because they really had no source or basis for enlightenment. In such an age of warring nobles against the kings and jealous rising classes in new cities, Marshal de Saxe pointed out that the military draft would have forced "the whole fabric of society to be rent from top to bottom." [4] But in the enthusiasm of the French Revolution, equality and fraternity won out over liberty. According to the theory of "a nation at arms" espoused by the Estates General in 1789

> Young men go to battle, married men forge arms, women make tents and clothing and the aged preach hatred of kings and the love of the Republic.[5]

Democracy without the emphasis on the complete rights of the individual and the freedom for minorities has remained at that very point ever since. Until now, no revolution has escaped the consequences of linking democracy as privilege with an awesome duty to the state which grants it, for no revolution has freed itself of primary loyalty to one nation-state. It is precisely here that the Soviet revolution was doomed from the beginning—even before Brest-Litovsk forced loyalty to fatherland ahead of faithfulness to the revolution. Marx was wrong to assume that socialism demanded an end to nationalism, or that it could not become the prisoner of a state that was incapable of withering away. As the votes of Marxists in the English and German parliaments during World War I were to show, the workingmen still had their countries.

Only in the nations with a British heritage do we need to qualify this. In England, despite dreadful impressment, conscription was never established as a principle.* Perhaps

---

* The Militia Acts were meant much more as a limitation on the King than as intentional conscription. They were never widely applied, and as they brought the first draft resistance from the Quakers, they were repealed in 1832.

this was partly due to the remaining anachronisms of aristocracy and monarchy. More probably, the reason is to be found in the largely bloodless nature of the middle-class revolution there. The original emphasis of individual freedom in the liberal writings of Locke and the French Enlightenment were retained far more frequently than in France, where the secondary importance of the state in the *contrat social* became the primary focus. England, too, soon put the libertarian doctrines to work for the new "liberal" causes, and individual freedom became less a bootstrap for the poor and much more a cover for the rich industrialist.

In America, the principle of individual freedom was the very basis of the most radical document ever written in connection with the founding of a state—the Declaration of Independence. Although compromised in the federal Constitution it came back to life in the Bill of Rights. The effect of slavery and the complete disregard for the rights of a whole race perhaps doomed the experiment from the start. But for a while, long after deTocqueville remarked on the broad possibilities of freedom in the new world, the land was large enough for both freedom and government. The west was Walden for generations of freedom seekers, and the end of the frontier was a crisis from which we have not recovered. Nevertheless, throughout our history and until very recently certain freedoms of the individual were not abridged—and one of these was freedom from conscription. The racial and economic crisis which provoked the Civil War led also to a brief interruption in our no-draft heritage. The crisis of becoming a "world leader" in the two world wars provoked other interruptions. Finally, the crisis of a bipolar world of armed camps after World War II altered the freedom system in many permanent ways; permanent peacetime conscription was one of these.

No real challenge (beyond the theoretical) to the validity of the nation-state arose until the 1920s in Europe. The boundaries had held, industrialism had progressed, fortunes had been made, a balance of power seemed to be working, and everywhere men were saying how nice the world was getting to be. The year 1900 saw almost universal optimism about the future of the human race—a rational future with neat divisions and balances and a slow dawning of plenty for all. "Democracy," or rule of the majority, within these separated nation-states, was seen as the efficient engine of this brighter world.

Then came the war to end all wars. However hopeful and extravagant the rhetoric of those who won that war, it was a rude shock from which the world has never recovered. New armaments, new machines of destruction on land and sea and in the air, blasted the balance and shattered the boundaries of European security in which America had shared the benefits. With the technological breakthroughs and the economic changes (not the least of which was the completion of industrialization) came new ideas as well. These refused to stop at border stations—they were carried by radio waves, smuggled through on trains, or dropped from planes in leaflet form. No new Peace of Westphalia could avert a new age of holy wars. Nothing could undo the impact of the Russian Revolution, though nationalized and partially contained. Fascism also crossed the world and brought perverse vitality to the attacks on the established order. A new international literature, art and philosophy sought to break forever the chains of convention and conformity which held the potential of the human spirit in check. The first reaches of modernism into Asia and Africa awoke the world to the brutality of enslavement and war on these continents which had proceeded almost unnoticed by Europe for five centuries during the slow conquest of the world by men of European stock. All progress and balance had to be viewed in a new light, when yellow and black people insisted upon the freedom and the necessities of existence that the "industrial democracies" of the west denied them.

America could ignore the new voices and try to forget just what really had happened in the woods of France. Europe could not forget, and particularly not Germany. Defeat there had meant the defeat of all the old ideas. The ideas of western democracy had been the vehicle for defeat and hence were as suspect as those of bureaucratic Prussia. Communism, fascism, existentialism and anarchism bloomed in the chaos after the war. Everything was questioned. As Karl Mannheim pointed out in *Ideology and Utopia,* written in the last days of Weimar Germany, this was no ordinary crisis in a political or social system, it was a thoroughgoing revolution in all values, challenging all interests and debunking everything. It was an "epistemological revolution," the likes of which have not been seen since the Sophist days of Socrates or the collapse of Rome. Reason and propriety were challenged along with political authority. Everything was illegitimate; no idea or institution was free of a hidden interest that needed to be exposed. The demonic side of this slap at reason and order was that it was used to establish an even more pervasive and perverse order of unreason. The Nazis in Germany tapped the anarchism and deep radicalism of the youth because no one else dared.

After the interruptions of World War II, in which all the champions of the status quo joined to defeat the demon challenger, and after a short-lived revival of the artificial ideological rivalry between old-style liberalism and national communism, the epistemological revolution returned with a fury. In art and music, the trends of the 1920s and 1930s toward disharmony and nonsense were introduced again, and the chaos was escalated. Dada became pop or op art, and the pessimistic nihilists and existentialists who had received so much attention in the dark days after Versailles were again to be found at the top of university bibliographies. It is scarcely an accident that the bittersweet anarchism of Hermann Hesse's *Demian* and *Steppenwolf* which had produced mass ecstasy in pre-Nazi Germany among the young became again a solace for many American college students in the 1960s. Whether in SDS or the civil rights movement, hippie culture or religious mysticism, the sons and daughters of the affluent managers of the rational, "democratic" nation-state called out to the children of all the other under-classes to join them in a new life.

Today's youth is no less human and therefore no less corruptible or capable of evil than any other generation. The desire of the young for freedom is as capable of being used for tyranny as was the last generation's desire for security. Except for one thing: it is new, and so far no established or disestablished authoritarianism has been able to capture its power. Whole generations of children are growing up in America and Europe, but also in the "developing nations" of the world, with the idea of freedom paramount in their minds. Something has destroyed their confidence in security as a desirable or reachable goal; something has made them question entirely the concept of total authority for the nation-state, for whatever reason—fighting communism or building it. This has even been true in the "socialist" world —Czechoslovakia could not have happened without the leadership and sacrifice of the youth.

Perhaps television, as McLuhan says, has played a major role. Never before have children been exposed to a hundred cultures and the rationale of a thousand conflicting interests in their living rooms. They have seen more sex, violence and political intrigue (real and unreal) than experienced or imagined by the most active adults of any previous generation. Perhaps the race question has revealed too many of the basic injustices on which our society has been built at home. From these influences it is but a step to realize other economic inequalities and to see that the whole democratic middle-class motherland has perpetuated and increased poverty and despotism in the colonies. The Vietnam war *has* been brought home for many young people, and with it the violence on which the state rests.

The youth ask the basic questions: Why are we killing and being killed in a war in a small nation so far away, why is there exploitation, why does not our society provide for the poor and the weak, why are the cities filled with hate and fear, why have basic services, housing and transportation broken down, why is America number one in medical technology yet among the most unhealthy nations of the world, why is alcoholism so rampant and largely unheeded yet youth who use marijuana are hounded and imprisoned, why are we poisoning our environment and murdering or maiming our children by the misuse we make of the air and water, why do our laws speak of freedom when the politicians' answer to more and more problems is "law and order" and police? And they will not be satisfied with answers revolving around either security or authority. The nation-state is no longer important to them and its security is meaningless aside from all of these other questions. Their loyalties are not yet firm, but they go beyond the border of the state and beyond the fringes of the class or status-group to which they belong by birth. Noam Chomsky has pointed to both the dangers and the positive potential of generations so enlightened yet so frustrated. On the one hand he fears their righteous indignation, if successful, could produce only more of the same.

One who pays some attention to history will not be surprised if those who cry most loudly that we must smash and destroy are later found among the administrators of some new system of repression.[6]

On the other hand he applauds the totality of their challenge.

To me it seems that the revival of anarchist thinking in the "New Left" and the attempts to put it into effect are the most promising developments of the past years, and that if this development can solidify, it offers some real hope that the present American crisis will not become an American and world catastrophe.[7]

To the war and the draft, and also to the state itself young people are saying, "Hell no, we won't go!" As this carries over into science and industry and into the bureaucracy itself, the true nature of the protest as one against the whole system of national security will become evident. Both for the future of the youth revolution as one of continuing emphasis upon freedom, honesty and hope, and for the sake of transforming the pressure of that movement into a political power to reconstruct America, it is important that youth and their allies realize early how great has been their impact and how worried is the power elite of our warfare state. Because youth challenge the right of the nation-state to define their goals, limit their visions or take their bodies and their lives, youth have almost universally said "no" to the draft. They have said "no" so firmly that the draft has been largely obstructed and effectively resisted as no other institution in our society. Perhaps 80,000 men have fled abroad, thousands have taken their cases to the clogged courts or are sitting in crowded jails, and other thousands have openly defied the law by destroying or turning in their draft cards. On June 10, 1970, over 12,000 draft cards were turned in to National Headquarters and a campaign was announced to solicit 100,000 more by fall. Many have gone unpunished because the state is helpless to deal with the disobedience of so many.

This unparalleled state of affairs has brought such a pressure on the government that it has studied every possibility for changing the conscription system. It hoped a new image and a new director would bring an answer, or that a muchtouted reform lottery would take the heat off, but in the last analysis it has been faced with only one possibility: ending the draft. Our government today responds only out of fear, a fear of situations that cannot properly be managed with bureaucratic and repressive procedures without causing a general breakdown in public trust. Young people have frightened the government on the subject of the draft. Although he will attempt to hold on to as much of the draft as possible (because its power is *his* power to wage war without Congress' approval) and to drag out the process of reform and abolition as long as he is able, the president now seems to have decided he *must* end the draft. He is not doing this because he is a party to the attack on the power of the violence experts. He is doing it in order to regroup the forces of national security behind other of the warfare institutions. His own aides have shown just how threatening is the draft to the government. Daniel P. Moynihan wrote the following in a memorandum to Mr. Nixon before the latter took office:

All we know is that the sense of institutions being legitimate—especially the institutions of government—is the glue that holds societies together. When it weakens things come unstuck. . . . Ending the draft would be the single most important step you could take [in order to] restore public confidence.[8]

Moynihan is worried because, as he points out, our own revolutionary heritage may give "the advantage to those who challenge authority." The Executive, of course, does not deal with the illegitimacy of our present institutions, or seek new ones to build legitimacy. He deals only with ways of gluing things back together. Sacrifice as little as possible, but when the attack becomes too potent, let some things go. The president has decided that, among those things, the draft can be abandoned.

But, without the draft, the president will be without a major tool for control at home and violence abroad. A major portion of that control at home has already been lost when the government yielded to pressures for an end to deferments. Deferments had been the chief way of manipulating and channeling American youth, and the success of "selective service" in using the poor and blacks for war while frightening the middle-class young into college, science, "defense industries" and teaching. Without deferments, the usefulness of the draft to the garrison state had been seriously impaired, although it remained a key device for Executive "flexibility" in foreign policy.* The fact that youth have forced the government to consider ending the draft is no mere strategic success; it represents their first real victory and should be seen as the first fruits of political power. Pressure can bring down presidents, but only power can change policies as basic as the draft. Instead of fearing to participate in the actual ending of the draft because the government has had to change its stand, the forces of freedom should seize it as a victory and take credit for it as a token of the rising power of people to call a halt to a runaway state.

---

* See Appendix for the domestic effects of channeling, and chapter 7 for the effects of the draft on foreign policy.

The end of the draft will prove that freedom is feasible. It will remove important powers from the president and the military. It can be used by youth and others who oppose the violence experts as a basis for new political power. It may provide a wedge in the military machinery for further popular control. The case for ending the draft is based neither on pure pacifism nor abstract anarchism; it is based solidly on the lost belief in individual freedom without which Americans will never get their nation back from those who seek to use it as a nuclear fortress and as the first token of a brave new world. In our world, nation-states armed to the teeth for national interest are as anachronistic as armored knights. There are no more nations, really, only empires and their protectorates, a whole world living in the shadows of holocaust and totalitarian giants. But freedom is feasible despite all that because its spirit has been revived among the young. What we propose is the American vision of Thoreau:

> There will never be a really free and enlightened State until the State comes to recognize the individual as a higher and independent power, from which all its own power and authority are derived, and treats him accordingly.[9]

The end of the draft is one step forward toward that goal.

NOTES

1. William O. Douglas, *The Right of the People* (New York: Doubleday, 1958), pp. 11–12.
2. Russell Kirk and James McClellan, *The Political Principles of Robert A. Taft* (New York: Fleet Press Corporation, 1967), pp. 77–78.
3. "The Real Case Against Conscription," *The Saturday Evening Post,* March 28, 1945, p. 17.
4. Theodore Ropp, *War in the Modern World* (Durham, North Carolina: Duke University Press, 1959), p. 38.

5. Richard D. Challener, *The French Theory of the Nation in Arms* (New York: Russ & Russ, Inc., 1965), p. 4. This book contains an excellent survey of the application of the theory consistently over 150 years of French history—and explains its utter failure under circumstances of twentieth-century war.
6. Noam Chomsky, *American Power and the New Mandarins* (New York: Random House, 1969), p. 18.
7. *Ibid.,* p. 19.
8. *The Evening Star,* Washington, D.C., March 11, 1970, p. 1.
9. Henry David Thoreau, *On the Duty of Civil Disobedience* (New York: Holt, Rinehart & Winston, 1960), p. 304.

Chapter 2

The State
and Its Citizens

Conscription is confiscation. It is the process wherein the established authority of a nation-state confiscates not the material property but the very lives of its citizens. Its purpose is to defend that established authority and the processes it represents.

By actual demonstration, the purpose cannot be the sentimental reverse, the protection of the citizens themselves. For one thing, the very act of conscription violates all the basic rights of the citizens. They must, in fact, give up the liberty which the conscription is propagandized to defend as the very first step in its process. The enemy waiting at the gate, supposedly, would at least have to win a great victory to end the liberty of the citizens. The act of conscription ends it for many without a shot being fired.

Ordinary laws are said to protect the rights of the citizen against overt acts against his person or property. They are laws which the citizen can obey simply by not acting *against* the laws (in short, by going about his life without bothering others). The law pertaining to conscription gives no such option. One cannot obey it by not interfering with the rights of others. One can obey it only by giving up *his* freedom and thenceforth acting on behalf of the state even if that action means taking the lives of others, invading the rights of others. It implies, in fact, acting without any regard to anything except the commands of the state.

That is what conscription does in action. It first takes the rights of the citizen away totally and then aims him, like a gun, at whatever target the state then chooses to destroy. Not once in the history of conscription, as Americans have known it, have the lives of citizens been confiscated simply to defend the homes and lives of those same citizens from attack. Instead, every conscription has seen the lives of the confiscated citizens ballistically delivered to an assault somewhere in the world against the established authority of some other nation-state.

The only exception to this in American history is the Civil War, although this may be viewed as an even more heinous use of conscription. While some soldiers undoubtedly believed that they were fighting on foreign soil, even more felt that they were being forced to fight against, if not brothers by blood, at least brothers by culture.

Even when the defense of confiscation conscription maintains, as it often and tellingly has, that the citizens were in fact being attacked, though indirectly and distantly, a case can be made against it. The confiscation of the lives of the citizens is accomplished by denying them even the right to decide whether or not they wanted to be defended in the first place.

There is no option in conscription, excepting only the very clouded one of objection on the basis of divine faith— an exception which in itself violates another ingrained part of the original social structure, at least the codified one, the separation of religious conscience from state affairs.

The majority-rule theory, also, fails when applied to this very distinct area. One idea of a democracy, such as supposedly was conceived here, is specifically to protect the minority from the murderous attention of the majority. The minority is compelled to bend to the will of the majority only in those matters which do not abridge the basic guarantees of the Bill of Rights. If a minority is bent to the majority will in a matter which clearly concerns the confiscation of its members' life and liberty and pursuit of happiness, then the minority has, in effect, no meaningful rights at all in the context of the majority.

None of this is idle opposition simply to the theory and practice of conscription. The basic points just made have been considered long and carefully by, for instance, the Supreme Court. The points have been considered and have been rejected—in deference to one other point which is the most significant of all points in the conscription issue. That is the paramountcy of the state and the secondariness of the citizen. The state may conscript only if it is viewed as having rights which precede those of the citizens, and that in its own defense it may sacrifice those citizens.

This hidden principle of state superiority shows why conscription *as a principle* is so basic a concern, and why even its temporary suspension would in no way resolve the questions behind it: of the nature of the state, the nature of citizenship, and the meaning of liberty in a land which has been said to have been conceived in it, but where the definition itself is a matter contended not only in the courts but on the streets.

The issue which is involved in conscription is the same issue involved in the riots, the protests, the tensions across the land, across the world, wherever established authority is being challenged—from the steps of the Kremlin to Capitol Hill. It is further tied to another challenge, the challenge to property relationships which modern America thought would never plague it, which Europe is attempting to compromise, and with which the Third World is grappling directly.

The problem still growing just beneath the surface of the conscription question is the question of property and the person and the relationship of both to the state—the final, full fleshing-out of the struggle between citizen and state. There is a striking difference between the way the state treats the person and the way it treats the property of certain persons. The state doesn't flinch from appropriating the person. It does not, however, treat inanimate property with the same summary disregard. Even when fighting what was officially regarded as a total war, the Second World War, the confiscation of property by the state was a matter of slow procedure, long struggle, many safeguards, lengthy litigation and, above all, was always accompanied by the notion of handsome indemnification.

The brief operation of railroads by the government, during the war and during a time of labor dispute, was such a felt distortion of the due processes of American law that it remains an object of study and wonder. The notion that American workers should abandon the secondary property right to strike during a "total" war also was resisted wholeheartedly and, in large measure, successfully.

In short, no rights pertaining to the industrial or commercial order have been consistently abrogated by this state, even in time of total war. But even in a time of no war, no emergency, no domestic defense, the quintessential rights of persons have been abridged. The specific justification is that the state is entitled to do anything in its self-defense. Given that, as the Supreme Court has, there is the question of what this particular state conceives of as the necessary "anythings," that is, what it truly considers to be its protective mission.

That mission, by definition and demonstration, is clearly not to protect the people who are the citizens of the state. They are confiscated. What then is left unconfiscated as the obvious and only thing that the state can be protecting? Property. The people are confiscated and they are sent to fight for something. The thing that is being fought for must be something which not only would be destroyed if not defended but which, during the defense, also is not being destroyed.

Since the people, the persons confiscated, easily may be destroyed, psychically by the confiscation itself, physically by the fighting that is at the end of that confiscation, they can scarcely be protected by the act of confiscation. Some of them are bound to be destroyed. On the other hand, property of various sorts is not destroyed by the process surrounding confiscation of the people. Indeed, property characteristically increases in value during that process. Property that might be destroyed, say, by an enemy action is not only compensated, but may be replaced. The life of the citizen, although compensated (but at a rate that is lower than that involved in the usual nonfatal traffic accident), cannot be replaced.

The Irish revolutionary leader, John Connolly, when his friends were threatened by conscription in the First World War, perceived such a distinction between persons and property in the process of conscription but, for polemic purposes perhaps, chose to turn it around to make a point.

> If it is right to take the manhood, it is doubly right to take the necessary property in order to strengthen the manhood in its warfare. . . . The conscription of the natural powers of the land and the conscription of the mechanical forces

[factory production] having been accomplished, the question of the conscription of the men to defend their new-won property and national rights may follow should it be necessary. But as the Irish state will then be in a position to guarantee economic security and individual freedom to its citizens, there will be no lack of recruits to take up arms to safeguard that national independence which they will see to be necessary for the perpetuation of both.[1]

Connolly did not live, of course, to see the bitter disappointment that, for instance, the Soviet Union, with its re-creation of a propertied and privileged class in the state bureaucracy would have represented to his socialistic ideals. He might have warmed, however, to the other factor cited in this discussion—that today's turbulent concern with these matters takes fully into account the relationship not only of propertied class to nonpropertied class but also the relationship of the state apparatus specifically in the defense of property whether old and stable or new and "revolutionary."

And it is precisely in the light of that relationship that the American system of conscription is being discussed here and throughout; in terms not of being a specific aberration in an otherwise different system but in terms of being essentially in and of a very specific system of property-person-state relationships. In the chapters on foreign policy, for instance, this is particularly clear when the issue becomes not one of whether, in some abstract way, a conscript military is needed to carry out any foreign policy, or protect it, but in a concrete way how a conscripted military is useful in carrying out the particular foreign policy of this particular modern industrial, corporate capitalist state.

To fail to study the draft from this vantage would be not only to accept the old dictum "my country, right or wrong," but also to lack curiosity as to the nature of "my country."

Neither seems in the disposition of this generation, to whom the nature of real things rather than the acceptance of abstractions is a preoccupation. In opposing the draft, of course, there are still those who simply say it is wrong, ignoring what it does and for whom and in what cause. Such opposition has been thoroughly gone over in the past. It now seems proper to look at the draft as part of the nation-state.

NOTES

1. *Workers' Republic*, January 15, 1916.

Chapter 3

The Kidnapped Dream

Observers of primitive societies have noted a special place for magic and myth. In ordinary life, everyday pursuits, men are not affected by them. It is only when faced with the extraordinary and, particularly, the dangerous that the magic is summoned and the myths raised as realities. And so it is in a highly refined way for advanced societies too. Men everywhere by and large have the common sense to conduct their ordinary affairs with decent, pragmatic regard for their neighbors, their environment, and the proportion of their own identity and projections. Endangered, or anticipating danger, they change. Myth and magic are summoned to their defense over the shards of their reason.

Of these myths and magical powers, none looms into the foreground more formidably than what Ernst Cassirer pointedly describes as "The Myth of the State." Common sense tells men that there is no such thing as the state, that it is a social invention so transparent that much history teaching is just trying to get people to remember the dates of the states that came and went and the names of the men who, as we all sometimes suspect, were the only reality of the state anyway. Again, in common sense, we know that all of those ancient battles were not fought to benefit just the abstractions of a state but rather the privileges of identifiable persons. Perhaps there is a sanity-seeking in the abstraction, however. How mad to think that so many died simply to aggrandize so few! Better perhaps to think of the great abstractions, like the state, rather than be left alone if even for a moment with the vision that all those graves were just the markers in what was very little more than a cosmic con game.

America's perception of the myth of the state and the dangers of its magic were, at the outset, so clear and so sharp that even in the midst of what was nothing less than a war of national liberation, the men fighting that war made explicitly clear, in their Declaration of Independence, that they saw the myth and beyond it to a hopeful reality.

The Declaration, in fact, was an epic document of history because it did dwell on the myth, shatter it, and define a reality. The Magna Carta, by contrast, had been a shopping list of immediate changes in certain social relationships. It didn't change a view of the world, it just changed the privileges of some people in that world.

The Declaration changed the view; it saw the state as mere mechanism, devoid of myth, a social invention which might be convenient at a given time and place and for a very limited purpose—a way, in fact, to organize protection of the people. And there was its genius. It saw the people as central and the state as *their* mechanism, and just a mechanism, no myth, no magic. It saw this so clearly, we must be reminded in these days of law and order, that it specifically enjoined the people to abolish governments regularly when they became more than mechanism and moved into myth and magic; that is, when they became more than protective devices and became, instead, ends in themselves, something beyond the reality of the citizens and their communities, something into the world where men could actually talk about national destiny and their country "right or wrong," saying things that would make them decently blush if they applied the same phrases to actual persons, things that are excusable only in the realm of the mystic.

The perception, the clear-sighted look beyond myth, didn't last long. It is possible to see in the Constitution, for instance, the end of the revolution, the end of the Declaration, and the beginnings of the state with all its attendant mythology. And this shift from reality to mythology, from the notion of the state as process-mechanism to the notion of state as institution, as *something,* involved just what the students of primitive societies had observed—a fear of events that made it necessary to reach beyond the rational.

Alexander Hamilton was haunted by such fears. He feared other, competitive nation-states and their commerce. He feared an America not aroused to compete in that commerce. He built the Federalist position upon them and he demolished the Declaration in doing it, planting the seed which grew into a state mythology that could excuse the confiscation of its citizens' lives simply in the name of the protection of the state.

It is useful to think of these things when thinking of conscription because of that crucial point, made earlier, that if people are made to give up their lives for the defense of a particular state then they should at least examine exactly what are the particulars of that state. Then, ultimately, they can even ask if they care to defend it. Or, alternatively, they can ask if there isn't some better way. At least they can, by looking the state squarely in the face, and not in the mirror of some highly polished legendary surface, begin the process of examining state decisions as something less than divinely inspired.

Hamilton's notion of the state contained both a frank view of the state as a mechanism to defend certain class interests and also as a part of a myth. The mechanistic, frank view was contained in his report on manufacturing which became the foundation for the victory of the Federalists, the central-power advocates, over the men who took the Declaration quite literally, feeling that government was an affair of local convenience, nothing more, and that the purpose of the revolution had been to free the people for their own destinies rather than to mold them into a great nation. Hamilton quite reasonably points out—as Stalin did later—that the nation could not quickly industrialize without a strong central government which commanded certain resources, including land, funds and franchises, and used them to create a capitalist class. When some asked, "Who needs them?" Hamilton's answer moved directly into mythology. The industrialization, and its capitalist class, was needed to make the state great. It was needed, in particular, to maintain an army and a navy of sufficient size as to assure that greatness.

The real situation was that the armies of the people, the forces that had beaten the greatest of all states, Great Britain, had just proven their efficacy. In short, the new nation already was great in the sense of armed strength, an armed strength that derived from the people themselves. But Hamilton needed something more compelling than just the vision of endless rows of factory stacks to inspire the victory for his Federalist position. He needed the sort of issue that could move the debate away from the common sense of the people at large and into a mystical realm that could justify class privilege, forced industrialization, abandonment of community in favor of nationhood, submergence of the individual into the collective state. He needed to introduce the element of fear which would do what it had always done in the past—make people suspend their good common sense and defer to the leadership of great men with great ideas.

The need to raise the army and the navy and the assumption that great armies and navies make great nations was based upon a form of fear: fear that always there would be barbarians at the gate, fear that whatever we had others would want so bad that they would rather fight for it than duplicate it. Great nations have always been described as nothing but the reflection of great armies and navies. The youngest child is taught that, from the time he opens his first history book or, rather, his first storybook about historical events. Revolutionaries sometimes emerge when children so raised begin to question in their own minds the difference between a great nation and a free people.

That question is essentially the question of legitimacy. We are born sensing that we are legitimate. That is, we are. The child is a squalling verification of legitimacy. He is hungry, therefore he exists. He knows that. Socially, *we* know that. It is his knowing it and our recognizing it that makes man what he is, that begins the epistemological process in which he explains himself. Somewhere along the line a person may be asked to transfer this notion of legitimacy to some other part of the social process. Commonly, it is to an institution.

Kenneth E. Boulding has devoted a wonderful mind

and a very special viewpoint to just this question as it pertains specifically to conscription. It is essential, in broadening the issue of the draft to something more than a discussion of one or another sets of legislation, to follow his fine reasoning in this regard. What follows is paraphrase (with some direct quotation) of one of his presentations on the subject.[1]

Most people tend to take legitimacy for granted. Particularly in the case of institutions that endure from one generation to the next, the next generation tends to accept what they have inherited as a social given. This is particularly true in regard to wealth and power.

Economists (wealth experts) rarely enquire into the legitimacy of exchange, even though this is the institution on which their craft is built. Political scientists (power experts) rarely probe the legitimacy of institutions of organized threat, such as the army or the police. (When they do, they too may be regarded as revolutionaries).

Yet, the dynamic of legitimacy is exactly the thing that allows permanent relationships to exist. When a man responds to an immediate threat, such as a gun pointed at his head, and hands over money to a thief, it is only a temporary basis. In order for a state tax collector to exact the money on a regular basis, somewhat peacefully, the same threat that the highwayman represented must be legitimatized into a process of government.

Legitimacy may be defined as general acceptance by all those concerned in a certain institution, role, or pattern of behavior that it constitutes part of the regular moral or social order within which they live. Thus legitimacy is a wider concept than the formal concept of law, even though the law is a great legitimator. At times, however, law itself may become illegitimate and when it does so its capacity to organize society is destroyed.[2]

Legitimacy has at least two dimensions—intensity and extent. Intensity is measured by the extent of sacrifice an individual is prepared to make for an institution rather than deny or abandon it. Extent is in the proportion of the relevant population that regards the institution as legitimate.

Legitimacy is nonlinear. The would-be conqueror is illegitimate at first. Then, if successful, legitimate. Then, after a certain point the process may sharply reverse so it is that

> at the greatest extent and power of a regime, nation, or empire that it often suddenly collapses through sheer loss of belief in it.[3]

As an example: the early years of the twentieth century found the concept of empire seemingly unshakable in its legitimacy. Yet in a few decades it was discredited, illegitimate, and collapsing even though two great ones remained afloat.

There may, indeed, be a critical moment at which the only way for an aging institution to retain legitimacy is to abandon power—as with monarchies becoming "constitutional," empires becoming commonwealths, and so forth.

At the present time by far the most wealthy, powerful and legitimate type of institution is the national state. In the socialistic countries the state monopolizes virtually all the wealth and the threat capability of the society. Even in the capitalist world the national state usually commands about 25% of the total economy and is a larger economic unit than any private corporation, society or church. Thus the United States government alone wields economic power roughly equal to half the national income of the Soviet Union, which is the largest socialist state. Within the United States government, the Department of Defense has a total budget larger than the national income of the Peoples Republic of China and can well claim to be the second largest centrally planned economy in the world. It is true that the great corporations wield an economic power roughly equal to that of the smaller socialist states; there are, indeed, only about 11 countries with a gross national product larger than General Motors. Nevertheless, when it comes to legitimacy the nation state is supreme. All other loyalties are expected to bow before it.

A man may deny his parents, his wife and his friends, his God or his profession and get away with it, but he cannot deny his country unless he finds another one.

In our world a man without a country is regarded with pity and scorn. We are expected to make greater sacrifices for our country than we make for anything else. We are urged, "Ask not what your country can do for you, ask what you can do for your country," whereas nobody ever suggests that we should "ask not what General Motors can do for you, ask what you can do for General Motors." An institution of such monumental wealth, power and legitimacy would seem to be invincible.[4]

But if history teaches anything it should teach us even at this moment of state invincibility to look most quizzically at the state. It may abound with conditions that will force it to abandon power in order to retain legitimacy or force it simply to collapse.

An institution which demands sacrifices can frequently create legitimacy for itself because of a strong tendency in human beings to justify to themselves sacrifices which they have made. We cannot admit that sacrifices have been made in vain.[5]

(It is obvious, of course, that the persistent prosecution of a war that has passed all ordinary bounds of understanding is justified solely on the basis of making sure that those who made the mistake, or the sacrifice, first shall not have died in vain—as though more error is better than the correction of the original error. That, too, is a critical example of the difference between the rational and the mythical or magical in political affairs.)

At some point, however, the sacrifices demanded by the institution simply become too great and a strain sets in.

> The real terms of trade between an individual and his country have been deteriorating markedly in the past decades. In the eighteenth century the national state made relatively few demands on its citizens, and provided some of them at least with fair security and satisfactory identity. As the nation has gathered legitimacy, however, from the bloodshed and treasure expended for it, it has become more and more demanding. It now demands ten to twenty percent of our income [the most current figure, actually, is thirty-six percent], at least two years of our life and it may demand the life itself, and it risks the destruction of our whole physical environment.
>
> As the cost rises, it eventually becomes not unreasonable to ask for what. If the payoffs are in fact low the moment has arrived when the whole legitimacy of the institution may be threatened.[6]

Boulding's speculation moves this along immediately to the question of the draft.

> The draft may well be regarded as a symbol of a slow decline in the legitimacy of the national state (or of what we should call more exactly the warfare state, to distinguish it from the welfare state which may succeed it), that slow decline which may presage the approach of collapse. In the rise and decline of legitimacy, as we have seen, we find first a period in which sacrifices are made, voluntarily and gladly, in the interests of the legitimate institution, and, indeed, reinforce the legitimacy of the institution. As the institution becomes more and more pressing in its demands, however,

voluntary sacrifices become replaced with forced sacrifices. The tithe becomes a tax, religious enthusiasm degenerates into compulsory chapel, and voluntary enlistment in the threatened system of the state becomes a compulsory draft.

The legitimacy of the draft, therefore, is in a sense a subtraction from the legitimacy of the state.

It represents the threat system of the state turned in on its own citizens, however much the threat may be disguised by a fine language about service and "every young man fulfilling his obligation." The language of duty is not the language of love and it is a symptom of approaching delegitimation. A marriage in which all the talk is of obligations rather than of love is on its way to the divorce court. The church in which all worship is obligatory is on its way to abandonment or reformation and the state in which service has become a duty is in no better case.

The draft therefore, which undoubtedly increases the threat capability of the national state, is a profound symptom of its decay and may hasten the day when people come to see that to ask "what can your country do for you" is a very sensible question.[7]

There is a view opened there that sees much farther than that question, of course. It looks to the historical point at which the entire institution under which the draft is subsumed either can be, should be, or must be questioned. It sees right back to the point of the conflict between the Declaration and the Constitution, back to the fork in the road where some men told us to resist even building a national state and others warned us that if we didn't we could never be great. Now that we are great, the question of the price of that greatness can be asked. We've bought the package; we can now read the fine print about its contents.

Boulding sees the question in somewhat less stark terms, preferring to say that it involves not the national state's very existence but simply the "unilateral national defense which supports it." [8] His study of the matter concludes:

> It seems clear therefore that those of us who have a genuine affection for the institution of the national state and for our own country in particular should constantly attack the legitimacy of the draft, and the legitimacy of the whole system of unilateral national defense which supports it, in the interest of preserving the legitimacy of the national state itself.
>
> The draft, it is true, is merely a symbol of a symptom of a much deeper disease, the disease of unilateral national defense, and it is this concept which should be the prime focus of our attack. Nevertheless, cleaning up a symptom sometimes helps to cure the disease, otherwise the sales of aspirin would be much less, and a little aspirin of dissent applied to the headache of the draft might be an important step in the direction of the larger objective. Those of us, therefore, who are realistically concerned about the survival of our country should probably not waste too much time complaining about the inequities and absurdities of the draft or attempt the hopeless task of rectifying it when the plain fact is that the draft can only begin to approach "justice" in time of major war, and a peacetime draft has to be absurd and unjust by its very nature. The axe should be applied to the root of the tree, not to its branches, and a little bug spray on the branches will not allay the rotteness of the trunk. An attempt to pretty up the draft and make it more acceptable may actually prevent that radical re-evaluation of the whole system of unilateral national defense which is now in order.
>
> We are very close to the moment when the only way to preserve the legitimacy of the national state will be to abandon most of its power. The draft is only a sub-plot in this much greater drama.[9]

Now if the only apparently questionable institution of the national state were this threat-method of confiscating

lives, the unilateral national defense which Boulding iden-
tifies, then the notion of "preserving" the legitimacy of the
national state might clearly involve just a change in that
defense system. Indeed, the latter half of this book dis-
cusses just such a change, or at least a mechanism toward
such a change. But Boulding has also described the problem with the national state at its level of highest myth and
magical content, the area in which it preaches the defense
of liberty by the very practice of denying it to its own
citizens.

The purely practical and far from magical level of the
operation of the national state remains—a level which is
enhanced by the operation of a warfare state whether that
state drafts citizens or not. The legitimacy issue is an echo of
the original struggle which Hamilton waged and won. Hamilton did not demand the strong national state just to raise
armies and navies (the myth-level of the "great" state,
the magic level of the wizards who preach that only by
being able to kill a maximum number of people can our
own particular part of the world be fit for life). He also
raised the pragmatic point of requiring a strong national
state to create a strong capitalist system and industrial
construction.

The purpose has been uninterrupted in all of our years.
The purpose of the nation has been to build industry. The
owners of that industry have been the direct beneficiaries
of that progress. The nonowners are benefitted indirectly,
as they have been under other state systems, by receiving
a wage for their labor power. A few even become actual
(not simply paper) owners themselves. Altogether, in a
very crucial sense, the owners, or what they own, represent
the class which the system will go to war to protect. If the
owners themselves have to join the fighting then they are
at least protecting something directly. The nonowners are

the people whose lives are confiscated and whose best hope at the end of the process is simply to have survived it all. Otherwise they leave the battle no better off than when they went in. Their property, which is their lives, is risked but not rewarded. Meantime, the material property of the owning class enhances steadily in value and, characteristically, also concentrates more and more in comparatively fewer and fewer hands. The facts of the equation are not often disputed but the meaning is. The conventional wisdom of the national state tells us that this is the way it should be and even adds that for the nonowning class a victorious war has at least accomplished even for them, even for the lowest of the low, the glowing freedom someday to become members of the owning class themselves.

To question the nature of the state is to question that conventional wisdom, and to question conscription, begins to move certainly in that direction. To question, even as Boulding has done, the notion of unilateral national defense is to question ultimately not just the legitimacy of the *idea* of the national state but also the nature of this particular nation state, the single most powerful and, with the Soviet Union, the most internationally interventionist nation state on the world stage today. (A recent document of the Senate for instance, lists 160 specific instances of armed U. S. intervention exclusive of declared wars!)

In the context of some nation-states—such as Sweden —it is possible to pursue the question of the draft, as Boulding has done, purely along the lines of the unilateral national defense system. By giving up the power to defend the state with a conscripted army it is eminently possible that Sweden can, as Boulding suggests, actually enhance the legitimacy of the national state itself. For the United States, which is not only a national state but an imperialist one as well, with a commitment to industrialization that has not wavered much since the time of Hamilton, giving up the power to conscript means very possibly giving up the power to *be* imperialist, to maintain an empire of interests and, with the strength of that far-flung empire, to continue a progressing course of industrialization.

By contrast, the Swedish state already had moved from warfare to welfare without causing much of a ripple in the world or pressures on its national style. For America to move, the entire world would have to move in response. To be sure, the possible stage of transition, in which the national state would give up the power to conscript but still retain the zeal to hire soldiers (see chapter 9) might well leave intact the hold on its empire of interests that America now has. It might even leave virtually intact the obeisance to national state power upon which the state must depend. It might even, again as Boulding suggests, give a boost to the national state's legitimacy. However, once the process by which the state confiscates lives is questioned, the questions about what those lives have been spent to protect might become too penetrating to be satisfied with the John Wayne movie answers which they have been given in the past, particularly in the public (national state) schools. If we abolish the draft, the question that was asked when the first American Revolution was being wrapped up in the Constitution of national state dominance might be asked again: why should men who want to be free accept the formation of a national state that simply seeks to be great, and which specifically defines that greatness in terms of factories and the armies needed to guard them in a quarrelsome world? In particular, what the questions of the confiscation of lives and the enhancement of property bring to mind is the terrifying possibility that all of the past sacrifices were made for a thing so valueless that people who thought they were free didn't care voluntarily to defend it.

General Hershey, the draft director, once told an audience at the National Press Club that he "hated to think of the day when my grandchildren might have to be defended by volunteers." General Hershey already had obviously lost faith in the dream that the history books talk about. War is, in that statement, just another business, requiring tight scheduling, production for production's sake, ways to get around competition. It is not, in that statement, the defense of a cause around which men of good will would rally on their own. That statement reduces the citizens to commodities, as indeed they are in the national state. Just as labor in the factory can be called simply a cost of production (not a contribution toward it, but a cost of it), lives in the defense of the national state can become just items of weaponry, precisely calculable as items of cost, certainly not voluntary or consensual. Not what is defended, but what is expended.

In that virtually cosmic statement of the man who had, for most of his adult life, operated the business of selecting men to be sent to die, is every echo of the arguments with which Hamilton had ended the dream of the Declaration of Independence or, rather, kidnapped it on behalf of a corporate America rather than a decentralized America. But whereas Hamilton had seen this great national state in the coldly calculating terms of forced industrialization, General Hershey's entire vocabulary moves into the world of myth and magic—the mythology of belonging to the state and the magic of fulfilling obligations to it, being ennobled thereby.

The national state seen at that point must be in trouble for all of the reasons cited by Boulding and more. For, as with primitive people, calling upon magic in the face of otherwise inexplicable phenomena, the national state seems driven in its extremity to defend itself by the rhetoric of what it hopes people will believe rather than by the reality of actually doing for them what the Declaration of Independence set out to do: safeguarding their life, liberty, and the pursuit of happiness.

And, to put it another way, the ghost that haunts it all is something else than having made so many sacrifices in vain. The ghost might well be that the sacrifices were made specifically to get what we have today. And the haunting question then is simply whether it was worth it. Since the system must live by confiscating the lives of some—cannibalism on a personal level—it's at least reasonable to ask the question.

The problem of the draft in this context, and in the meaning of that question, brings us back to the national state. It questions, of course, the legitimacy of the state's action in this particular regard, and it gives the state a chance to change its ways. But, to make again the point that cannot be made too often if more than the surface is to be scratched, if the thing is to be approached root and branch, is to make the point that cried to be made in so many past debates on the draft: it is the very nature of the national state itself, its entire corporate nature that is at issue.

The people have been asked so often to die for the national state. It is just possible that now the people may ask the national state to die, for the people.

NOTES

1. Kenneth E. Boulding "The Impact of the Draft on the Legitimacy of the National State," *The Draft,* ed. by Sol Tax (Chicago: University of Chicago Press, 1967).

2. *Ibid.*, pp. 191–192.
3. *Ibid.*, p. 192.
4. *Ibid.*, p. 193.
5. *Ibid.*, pp. 193–194.
6. *Ibid.*, p. 194.
7. *Ibid.*, p. 195.
8. *Ibid.*, p. 194.
9. *Ibid.*, p. 196.

Chapter 4

The Conscripted Mind

Conscription has abolished the social concept of the individual in this national state. Just as the factory system changed workers from persons to personnel, and just as representative democracy turned the participating citizen of the town meeting into the statistical voter of the network computer, so did conscription turn the citizen-soldier defending his home into the military manpower-procurement problem of the technicians defending the national state on the battlefield and, most strikingly, behind it.

If this were simply the dispeptic conclusion of a social critic it would at least be worth some examination to determine the remote possibility of its truth. In the early history of the country, the idea itself of conscription was debated. It is a significant measure of changed attitudes that for several generations the debate hasn't been on whether the system should exist at all but simply about its "fairness." Further, and crucially significant, the conceptualization of conscription as a conscious manpower-channeling device of the national state comes not from critics but is an ingrained, explicit, promulgated policy of the national state itself.

If, indeed, this particular national state has written any definitive declaration of its purposes, that declaration might well be the Selective Service System's statement on channeling which was issued in July 1965, and withdrawn from circulation as soon as it was discovered having leaked to light.* Yet it has never been rescinded in application or intent. While the barons had their Magna Carta and while the dreamers of a free society had their Declaration of Independence, the practitioners of the national state's total bureaucracy have their memo on channeling. It is because it is *that* significant that it is reviewed, portion by portion, here.

Its Preamble is striking:

> One of the major products of the Selective Service classification process is the channeling of manpower into many endeavors, occupations and activities that are in the national interest.

With millions dead in the long struggle toward emancipation of man from ownership and exploitation by other men, with at least three major modern revolutions having been bloodily fought because men contested being owned and exploited, with a world ablaze today over precisely that issue, it is the anonymous pen of an anonymous bureaucrat that matter-of-factly reminds us of the *realpolitik*: the fact that in the United States of the latter half of the twentieth century, it is possible for a fourth- or fifth-

---

* See Appendix for full text of this memorandum.

generation son of revolutionary America to speak blandly of people who might regard themselves as citizens as nothing but manpower which must be "channeled" into slots which are in the "national" interest.

The shift from citizen to "manpower" is surely as significant as the shift from worker or person to personnel. The assumption that the national interest no longer has anything to do with serving the people, but now has to do only with the people serving the state is, in politics, the quantum leap from free man to subject.

There is another way to gauge the heavy impact of what is just the opening of the Selective Service System's most definitive statement on its broad role in the society. Consider what other state documents would be abrogated if the channeling memo were, for instance, to become an openly legal document, a federal law. This is not to say that as a law it would have any greater effect, but simply to suggest what its openly legal status would mean.

First, the Declaration of Independence is altogether abrogated by the channeling memo. The Declaration holds that the purpose of the government is to protect the rights of the citizens but, further, that it is the primary responsibility of the citizens themselves to protect those same rights against encroachment by the government. The channeling memo clearly states that the primary rights in the society are those of the state (national interest having no other sensible meaning in this context) and that in the service of that interest the state has the specific right to move people into such "endeavors, occupations and activities" as best suits its and not their purposes. So much for the American Revolution.

What about the Constitution? Even that document, although it primarily cedes rights to the state and takes them away from the people, at least draws the line at a provision granting a power to conscript. Ever since, of course, it has been argued by some that the power to "raise" armies and navies is the same thing. It has just as strenuously been argued in opposition that the power to raise the money with which to raise the armies is far from the same thing as having the power to grab the bodies. And others can correctly add that bodies with money don't get grabbed. But in that section of the Constitution actually concerned with individual rather than state's rights, the Bill of Rights, there is an unremitting spirit of opposition to the sort of autocratic, arbitrary assumption of power evidenced in the channeling memo. The Ninth Amendment, for instance, carefully points out that the grants of power specifically *enumerated* (not hinted) in the Constitution "shall not be construed to deny or disparage others retained by the people." Since the Constitution does not enumerate the right to channel people among the rights granted to the state, then the right to follow "endeavors, occupations and activities" of one's own choice, and not the state's, is a Ninth Amendment right retained by the people.

Apparently even the author of the channeling memo was aware that there might be some piddling concern about the way in which the Selective Service System had burgeoned, in his memo, from merely military manpower to a system of national manpower. The concern becomes evident in the next paragraph:

> The line dividing the primary function of armed forces manpower procurement from the process of channeling manpower into civilian support is often finely drawn.

Being a proper spokesman for the realities of state power, however, the author then proceeds to give a very good and pragmatic reason why the line doesn't count. He shows, in fact, the inevitable development of the state's power to confiscate life for purely military reasons into its ability to confiscate the citizen's choices for paramilitary reasons.

The process of channeling by not taking men from certain activities who are otherwise liable for service, or by giving deferment to qualified men in certain occupations, is actual procurement by inducement of manpower for civilian activities which are manifestly in the national interest.

To proceed backward on that, we note first the escalation of rhetoric from plain old national interest to a manifest national interest. In that may be the first chilling suggestions that it no longer requires a directive from Washington to tell the people what the national interest is. Instead, the education to citizenship has been so successful that bureaucrats now can safely rely on the notion that what they see as the national interest is going to be manifestly apparent to everyone else as well. Next there is the candid recognition that when the government so uses its power, it is not simply inducement or suggestion but "actual procurement" that takes place. And, of course, that is very much the case. The discretionary words about "certain" activities and "certain" occupations, and the value judgment by which men in those spheres are called "qualified," heighten the point that the state is not only the owner of the so-called citizens but is the arbiter of their worth and, further, the evaluator of their pursuits.

In full exposition of just how well the state's technicians have thought all of this out, and in further full exposition of the fact that this particular statement is no casual exercise but a reasoned declaration of state power, the channeling document spells out in some detail the practical effect of its meaning.

While the best known purpose of Selective Service is to

procure manpower for the armed forces, a variety of related processes take place outside delivery of manpower to the active armed forces.

Again note, along the way, the commodity concept of the person who is not only transformed into manpower but also is "delivered" to the active armed forces of the state.

Many of these may be put under the heading of "channeling manpower." Many young men would not have pursued a higher education if there had not been a program of student deferment. Many young scientists, engineers, tool and die makers, and other possessors of scarce skills would not remain in their jobs in the defense effort if it were not for a program of occupational deferments.

Note the implicit suggestion that citizens in sufficient number could not be expected voluntarily to work even in civilian jobs related to defense were it not for the *threat* of having to serve that effort even more directly in the active armed forces. Throughout the official thinking of the Selective Service there is this implicit notion of the national interest—defense as requiring force to make people serve it.

Even though the salary of a teacher has historically been meager, many young men remain in that job, seeking the reward of a deferment.

What that seems to say is simply that anything, *even* a job in a school, is viewed as preferable to serving the national interest—defense.

The process of channeling manpower by deferment is entitled to much credit for the large number of graduate students in technical fields and for the fact that there is not a greater shortage of teachers, engineers and other scientists working in activities which are essential to the national interest. . .

The System [their capitalization] has also induced needed people to remain in these professions and in industry engaged in defense activities or in the support of national health, safety or interest.

What begins to emerge is a sort of nightmare world in which graduate studies would not be pursued, science not advanced, pupils not taught if it were not for the threat which the state holds over the people and which it wisely uses to accomplish what the people themselves would not, i.e., science, teaching, etc. Also repeated is the pessimistic theme that the defense of the nation-state or, indeed, even the health and safety of the national state, and presumably the people who inhabit its domain, would be devoid of talent if not for the threat, if not for the "inducement" held out by the blatant deal of making people serve some civilian part of the national interest or else be subjected to what must be considered the worst of all forms of service, armed service. This cynical view in this cynical in-house paper contrasts vividly, of course, with the propagandist's view that the *highest* form of loyal service to the national state is armed service. Children are taught this in various films and storybooks but, obviously, even the Selective Service System does not wholly believe that the lessons have been effective enough to risk voluntarism. And, to bring that notion full circle, there is the same sort of pessimism about people voluntarily doing *any* sort of work which would serve the national interest, that great, gray undefined abstraction, without being induced to do so by the threat of armed servitude. That this seems to contradict the earlier notion of "manifest" national interest may be more a confusion as to where we stand than as to where we are going.

The SSS memo on channeling continues with an elaboration of the thinking behind the bonus effects of draft deferments.

This was coupled with a growing public recognition that the complexities of future wars would diminish further the distinction between what constitutes military service in uniform and a comparable contribution to the national interest out of uniform. Wars have always been conducted in various ways, but appreciation of this fact and its relationship to preparation for war has never been so sharp in the public mind as it is now becoming. The meaning of the word "service," with its former restricted application to the armed forces, is certain to become widened much more in the future. This brings with it the ever increasing problem of how to control effectively the service of individuals who are not in the armed forces.

And there it is. All out in the open, all perfectly candid. There is, first of all, a reasoned acceptance of the fact that the United States is a warfare state. There is no contextual or other sort of hint that the notion of preparation for war is a sometime thing or is, indeed, part of an actual emergency. Remember, this memo was issued in 1965 when even the Vietnamese war was officially considered manageable and when the victorious presidential candidate had promised that it would end soon and certainly not escalate. But in this memo as, obviously, in the state altogether, the line between war and war preparation is consciously erased as is the notion that men in uniform are the only soldiers in the national state's defense. But looming above it all is the statement of THE PROBLEM: "how to control effectively the service of individuals who are not in the armed forces."

The equation is now numbered out precisely. The state's interest, the national interest, is paramount. All of the citizens are subordinate to that interest. Where war once was fought by soldiers, now it must be fought by all. Citizens must be induced to become part of that all, to serve specifically in the specific locations and modes of interest to the state. The condition of war itself is no longer the determining factor as to when this new concept of service is owed to the state. Now the state must also prepare for war regularly, and with a rational grasp of all the resources available. One of those resources which constitutes an increasing problem is the service of persons who are not in uniform and who, therefore, cannot be commanded by military fiat but *must* be at the command of the state in some new social modality.

The new philosopher of the new and total service state muses on in his memo.

In the Selective Service System the term "deferment" has been used millions of times to describe the method and means used to attract to the kind of service considered to be most important, the individuals who were not compelled to do it. The club of induction has been used to drive out of areas considered to be less important to the areas of greater importance in which deferments were given, the individuals who did not or could not participate in activities which were considered essential to the defense of the Nation. The Selective Service System anticipates further evolution in this area.

The perceptive reader can answer these questions about that part of that memo: Who is it who decides which areas are important? Who decides which individuals may or may not be compelled to armed service? Who decides which are to be channeled into other service? What is induction considered to be, an honor or a club? How must the citizens of the republic be moved, by agreement or by being driven? Who or what is being defended, the people or the "Nation?" What is the growth area for the expansion of the principles and practices and bureaucracy of conscription? How would you describe the set of mind that views men as this statement views them? How would you describe the "Nation" that so sees its citizens? How would you describe a citizen who would agree to service in that kind of nation?

The memo then shifts for a moment into the pragmatic area of just how the people shall be driven to do what the "Nation" decides is in its best interests:

> No group deferments are permitted. Deferments are granted, however, in a realistic atmosphere so that the fullest effect of channeling will be felt, rather than be terminated by military service at too early a time.
>
> Registrants and their employers are encouraged and required to make available to the classifying authorities detailed evidence as to the occupations and activities in which the registrants are engaged. . . . Since occupational deferments are granted for no more than one year at a time, a process of periodically receiving current information and repeated review assures that every deferred registrant continues to contribute to the overall national good. This reminds him of the basis for his deferment.

Pragmatic and firm. The classifying authority, as agent of the national state, now joins with the factory owners to keep tabs on the workers, to be sure that they are doing good work in good causes, causes certified by the agent of the state as part of the overall collaboration between the businessmen of the nation and the bureaucrats of the nation. Further, the classifying authority, as agent for the state, takes this opportnuity also to remind everyone involved who the boss really is, where the power lies, and by whose good will and consent men are permitted to do whatever they are doing.

From the pragmatic, the memo shifts suddenly to the

philosophical with a magical mystery tour of the national state's chief source of legitimation: patriotism.

Patriotism is defined as "devotion to the welfare of one's country." It has been interpreted to mean many different things. Men have always been exhorted to do their duty. But what their duty is depends upon a variety of variables, most important being the nature of the threat to national welfare and the capacity and opportunity of the individual. Take, for example, the boy who saved the Netherlands by plugging the dike with his finger.

At the time of the American Revolution the patriot was the so-called "embattled farmer" who joined General Washington to fight the British. The concept that patriotism is best exemplified by service in uniform has always been under some degree of challenge, but never to the extent that it is today. In today's complicated warfare, when the man in uniform may be suffering far less than the civilians at home, patriotism must be interpreted far more broadly than ever before.

This is not a new thought, but it has new emphasis since the development of nuclear and rocket warfare. Educators, scientists, engineers and their professional organizations, during the last ten years particularly, have been convincing the American public that for the mentally qualified man there is a special order of patriotism other than service in uniform —that for the man having the capacity, dedicated service as a civilian in such fields as engineering, the sciences and teaching constitute the ultimate in their expression of patriotism. A large segment of the American public has been convinced that this is true.

Emergent in that section, implicitly, is the elitism of the state philosophy. Those who may give only their bodies, because they are stupid, must of course give those bodies. But there is now a higher order of patriotism for that higher order of man—the technocrat in the service of the bureaucrats—and thanks to a healthy propagandizing that higher order of patriotism has become an accepted part of American life. (No wonder that—as will be subsequently discussed—so few question the largely black army in Vietnam. After all, what have *they* to offer but their bodies? The white sons of the white middle class and the better schools will give, instead of their bodies, their "superior" minds to the Nation.) Patriotism.

It is in this atmosphere that the young man registers at age 18 and pressure begins to force his choice. He does not have the inhibitions that a philosophy of universal military service in uniform would engender. The door is open for him as a student if capable in a skill badly needed by his nation. He has many choices and he is prodded to make a decision.

The psychological effect of this circumstantial climate depends upon the individual, his sense of good citizenship, his love of country and its way of life. He can obtain a sense of well-being and satisfaction that he is doing as a civilian what will help his country most. This process encourages him to put forth his best effort and removes to some degree the stigma that has been attached to being out of uniform.

It is to be expected that men involved in the profound remaking of a republic into a state at the center of an empire should become harassed by contradictions and inconsistencies from time to time. Thus, the club of conscription now becomes an honor so great that those who do not share it might be stigmatized. Also there is the exhaled breath, as in a sigh, when we realize how clumsy it would have been to have universal military service—as once was experimentally tried—because this would not take into account the modern reality: that an armed state, a Warfare Nation, is a far bigger and better thing than the old crude concept of a state with merely a large army. Absolutely consistent, however, is the paragraph's reiteration of the idea that it is only by service to the state that man can achieve high satisfaction and a sense of well-being. That is the standard of the new national state regnancy.

But what of the churl who does not come equipped with good national state reflexes? Well, there is even hope for him because the state will not let him fall too deeply into the sloth of his ways.

In the less patriotic and more selfish individuals it engenders a sense of fear, uncertainty and dissatisfaction which motivates him, nevertheless, in the same direction.

He complains of the uncertainty which he must endure; he would like to be able to do as he pleases; he would appreciate a certain future with no prospect of military service or civilian contribution, but he complies. . . .

Throughout his career as a student, the pressure—the threat of loss of deferment—continues. It continues with equal intensity after graduation. His local board requires periodic reports to find out what he is up to. He is impelled to pursue his skill rather than embark upon some less important enterprise and is encouraged to apply his skill in an essential activity in the national interest. The loss of deferred status is the consequence for the individual who has acquired the skill and either does not use it or uses it in a nonessential activity.

Suffice it to say that in the very next paragraph this reign of terror, this definition of the citizen wholly in terms of his service to the state, this unremitting vista of a future always full of such fear and such service, this bleak landscape of the total state and the totally conscripted "citizen," is described with probably horrifying accuracy as "the American way."

The psychology of granting wide choice under pressure to take action is the American or indirect way of achieving what is done by direction in foreign countries where choice is not permitted. Here, choice is limited, but not denied, and it is fundamental that an individual generally applies himself better to something he has decided to do rather than something he has been told to do.

The choice, of course, already has been defined as between service in or out of uniform, not whether or not to serve. The lack of choice, as a matter of fact, in those countries-of-no-choice to which the memo refers means at worst assignment by the state to serve. Whether it is in or out of uniform just doesn't make any difference. Also implicit in the Selective Service System memo is the justification of the American way of limited-pressure choice as being not more just, but simply more efficient. The idea of limited choice as the best motivator of manipulated men was exactly the idea used by the National Socialists of Germany in their first experiments with extermination camps. At Treblinka, for instance, docility of the victims was assured by permitting them apparent choices in such matters as which turn to take at certain road forks—which eventually met at the same place—and in selecting assignments which, by offering choices, restored a feeling of hope among the prisoners, even though each and every one was doomed no matter what choice he might make at any given time, or whether that choice might slow or speed his course toward the gas chamber by a day or two. By much the same reasoning of the Selective Service System memo on channeling one might conclude that the Jews and others who died in the gas ovens were—by the national state's standards—contributing their fullest measure of devotion to the interests of the nation, the welfare of the state.

Again, after a dip into the metaphysics of the state, the Selective System memo returns to homey example to bring its case back down to earth:

The effects of channeling are manifested among student physicians. They are deferred to complete their education through school and internship. This permits them to serve in the armed forces in their skills rather than in an unskilled capacity as enlisted men.

The device of pressurized guidance, or channeling, is employed on Standby Reservists of which more than 2½ million have been referred by all services for availability determinations. The appeal to the Reservist who knows he is subject to recall to active duty unless he is determined to be unavailable is virtually identical to that extended to other registrants.

Very simply, make the most of the meat on the hoof. Why settle for a bunch of enlisted hamburger when you can get professional sirloins? Also, of course, there is the interesting notion that even a reservist would prefer to work anywhere, doing anything the state finds useful rather than go into active service. This observation makes the entire concept of the Reserve something a bit less heroic than the recruiting posters would have it.

The memo then turns to a curious dilemma the SSS and the nation face in regard to the citizens who get away:

> The psychological impact of being rejected for service in uniform is severe. The earlier this occurs in a young man's life, the sooner the beneficial effects of pressured motivation by the Selective Service System are lost. He is labeled unwanted. His patriotism is not desired. Once the label of "rejectee" is upon him all efforts at guidance by persuasion are futile. If he attempts to enlist at 17 or 18 and is rejected, then he receives virtually none of the impulsion the System is capable of giving him. If he makes no effort to enlist and as a result is not rejected until delivered for examination by the Selective Service System at about age 23, he has felt some of the pressure but thereafter is a free agent.

When the memo refers to the "severe" psychological impact it is tempting, perhaps, to think that it might refer to the trauma felt by the poor fellow who is rejected for service and who, for his own reasons, feels this is a blight upon his life. But no. The paragraph makes repeatedly clear that the severe impact that concerns the SSS is the impact on their ability to apply "pressured motivation" to the person. The concern becomes transparent when it is mentioned that the impacted person with the "rejectee" label seared upon his soul is 1) impervious to persuasion, making one wonder why he wouldn't be dying, rather, to prove his patriotism by taking the meanest defense job available, and 2) is a *free agent*. The psychological impact is now clear. It is the impact of being a free agent that is the trauma the SSS fears. And why not? Would free agents serve the warfare state the way that the state's manpower procurement office feels they should? The answer lies in the inescapable paradox: if patriotism is the high virtue, and widely spread one, that the SSS feels it to be, then why worry about manipulating people? Shouldn't patriots, as a matter of fact, just be waiting to be told they are needed to serve, rather than having to be tracked down and forced to do it? If there was even a trace of truth to the SSS's notion that young people do not want to feel "unwanted" then, of course, being rejected from service would not be, as it is, one of life's brass rings for most young people— and enlistments would be so great as to flood the barracks of the land.

With a practical eye, however, the SSS memo shows that it has even found a way to get around the possibility of a lot of smug people going around feeling unwanted for military service.

This contributed to establishment of a new classification of I-Y (registrant qualified for military service only in time of war or national emergency). That classification reminds the registrant of his ultimate qualification to serve and preserves some of the benefit of what we call channeling. Without it or any other similar method of categorizing men in degrees of acceptability, men rejected for military service would be left with the understanding that they are unfit to defend their country, even in wartime.

The contradiction, mentioned earlier, which says at one time that service is an honor and then that it is a menace richly applies here. Earlier, it will be recalled, much of America had been described as agreeing that service out of uniform not only could be as good as service in uniform but as a matter of fact could be even superior. Now, however, it seems that a person not permitted to serve in uniform is socially deformed beyond recognition. Where then the separate but equal honor of being patriotic in a classroom, a lab, or a factory? Perhaps it is just an old bias, considering that the Selective Service System is, despite the neighborhood boards, completely dominated by military personnel and military standards. It is, in fact, the warfare state in action.

The paragraph that follows seems mostly a bureaucratic staking-out of jurisdiction rather than a profound addition to the philosophy of the memo.

An unprejudiced choice between alternative routes in civilian skills can be offered only by an agency which is not a user of manpower and is, therefore, not a competitor. In the absence of such an agency, bright young men would be importuned with bounties and pirated like potential football players until eventually a system of arbitration would have to be established.

After that, back to the nitty gritty.

From the individual's viewpoint, he is standing in a room which has been made uncomfortably warm. Several doors are open, but they all lead to various forms of recognized, patriotic service to the Nation. Some accept the alternatives gladly—some with reluctance. The consequence is approximately the same.

All of the previously mentioned points about state control are evident again, of course, but even more evident is the style, in which human beings are discussed with precisely the terms and coldness an experimenter with rats might use to describe their meanderings through mazes and their reactions to the rewards of food and the punishments of electrical shocks. Undoubtedly, experiments with rats in "uncomfortable" rooms and with several doors open to them have been recorded. Should those doors enter only upon similarly depressing rooms then the results probably have been recorded also. They can be imagined: frustration, anguish, self-destruction.

The memo then moves from the philosophical to the practical.

> The so-called Doctor Draft was set up during the Korean episode to insure sufficient physicians, dentists, and veterinarians in the armed forces as officers. The objective of that law was to exert sufficient pressure to furnish an incentive for application for commission. However, the indirect effect was to induce many physicians, dentists and veterinarians to specialize in areas of medical personnel shortages and to seek outlets for their skills in areas of greatest demand and national need rather than of greatest financial return.

At one level that is one of the strongest boosts for socialized medicine ever given by a state agency. At another level, however, it also reveals that it is the warfare state, and not the welfare state that remains the prime objective of the socialized state objectives of the Selective Service System.

The concluding paragraphs of the memo are simply presented here without comment for they are clear enough in their naked dress. Beginning with nothing more nor less than an implied sanction of the goals of state socialism (centralized, as opposed to peoples', socialism), it quibbles only about technique.

Selective Service processes do not compel people by edict as in foreign systems to enter pursuits having to do with essentiality and progress. They go because they know that by going they will be deferred.

The application of direct methods to effect the policy of every man doing his duty in support of national interest involves considerably more capacity than the current use of indirection as a method of allocation of personnel. The problem, however, of what is every man's duty when each individual case is approached is not simple. The question of whether he can do one duty better than another is a problem of considerable proportions and the complications of logistics in attempting to control parts of an operation without controlling all of it (in other words, to control allocation of personnel without controlling where people eat, where they live and how they are to be transported), adds to the administrative difficulties of direct administration. The organization necessary to make the decisions, would, of necessity, extract a large segment of population from productive work. If the members of the organization are conceived to be reasonably qualified to exercise judgment and control over skilled personnel, the impact of their withdrawal from war production work would be severe. The number of decisions would extend into billions.

Deciding what people should do, rather than letting them do something of national importance of their own choosing, introduces many problems that are at least partially avoided when indirect methods, the kind currently invoked by the Selective Service System, are used.

Delivery of manpower for induction, the process of providing a few thousand men with transportation to a reception center, is not much of a challenge. It is in dealing with the other millions of registrants that the System is heavily occupied, developing more effective human beings in the national interest. If there is to be any survival after disaster, it will take people, and not machines, to restore the Nation.

The temptation is to take this memo as somehow an aberration rather than a characteristic of the American state as it has developed in its full course away from participatory to "representative" (delegated) democracy, away from the spirit of a people's country as envisioned in the Declaration of Independence, and toward a national state. To follow the temptation would be a complacent mistake. Parse the Selective Service System memo along with the speeches of major politicians and the same style of state nationalism comes clearly through.

There is John Kennedy's famed "ask not what your country can do for you, ask instead what you can do for your country." Echoing that there is another political statement which says the same thing in a less poetic manner: "Instead of . . . society for the individual, we have the individual for society." Isn't that the same as the Kennedy definition of state nationalism? It is by Alfredo Rocco, in what Benito Mussolini himself referred to as a definitive presentation of the doctrine of fascism.[1]

Compare this apotheosis of what the Selective Service System wants to do:

> [The state leader] must take an activist view of his office. He must articulate the Nation's values, define its goals and marshal its will.

with the following.

> [The state leader] sets up the great ends which are to be attained and draws up the plans for the utilization of all na-

tional powers in the achievement of the common goals . . . he gives the national life its true purpose and value.

The first quotation is from Richard M. Nixon, just before his election as President, describing the role of the Chief Executive.[2] The second is from Ernst Rudolph Huber's *Constitutional Law of the Greater German Reich*.[3] It describes the state leadership role of Adolph Hitler.

Both statements find their practical, workaday mechanism in the memo of the Selective Service System on how the human cattle of the state are to be channeled and herded into the stalls of the national interest.

NOTES

1. "The Political Doctrine of Fascism," a speech by Alfredo Rocco given at Perugia, translated, along with Mussolini's comments, in *Readings on Fascism and National Socialism,* Department of Philosophy, University of Colorado (Boulder: Swallow Press).
2. Speech made in London, Ohio, October 22, 1968.
3. Verfassungsrecht des grossdeutschen Reiches, Berlin, 1939. Contained in *Readings in Fascism and National Socialism, op. cit.*

Chapter 5

The Impacted Group

Seen from the very top, from the Selective Service System bureaucracy itself, conscription has carved the nation's male population into roughly two groups: the group with no particular skill, or with skills not needed by the nation, and the group with skills needed by the nation in factory, on farm, in classroom, office, or laboratory. But in those groups are subsumed many others and the impact of conscription upon them is deadly.

In October, 1969, the National Council on Family Relations analyzed publicly available data to find those groups and to try and understand the effect upon them and the rest of us of conscription's current major project, the war in Vietnam. That the study can be considered a study of the impact of conscription and not just the war is supported by the fact that the Selective Service people themselves, as well as most other officials of the Department of Defense who speak publicly on the matter, all agree that without

conscription we would be having a war for which few
people would be showing up, at least too few to fight it
the way the warriors and their political leaders want to
fight it. The system may be said to make the war possible
at this time rather than the other way around.

First, of course, there is the age group most severely
impacted by conscription and subsequently by the toll on
the battlefield. The ages of the men actually involved in
the fighting range from seventeen to fifty-one but ninety percent of the casualties are among men under twenty-six and
seventy-five percent of the casualties are in the nineteen to
twenty-three age group. It means that a group that represents about five percent of the male population in the
United States bleeds and dies far and away more than
any other. War can be seen in that sense as a young man's
burden imposed by old men's mistakes.

One of the favorite pastimes of those same old men in
minimizing the cost of their wars is to tell us that, after
all, we kill more people in traffic accidents. Harry Truman,
for instance, shrugged off the Korean War that way. There
are both moral and statistical comments to be made on that
equation. Morally, of course, "we" don't kill those people
in traffic accidents. Certain drivers do, or certain pedes-
trians. And when it comes to war, "we" may docilely obey
the decisions but it is "they" who make them.

Statistically, the Council on Family Relations has this
to say about the auto accident rationalization of killing so
many young people:

> Looking at Vital Statistics Mortality tables for 1966 (pub-
> lished 1968) we can estimate an increase in the overall death
> rate for the hardest-hit cohort (20–25 males) of 50% for
> the period 1966–68, and 100% for 1968 alone, when battle
> deaths numbered 14,592 [the present total is about 40,000].
> Ordinarily, civilian death rates in this age group are low,

about half accounted for by automobile accidents. For this age group, then, the Vietnam toll assumes epidemic proportions for death and injury.[1]

In short, we may lose more people in traffic accidents, but not more young people. They pay the extra fare for the power trip of war.

It is true, however, that feeding a war such as the one in Vietnam does not deplete the raw material of the state— available bodies—so fast that the depletion alone causes grave concern. The state, it could be said, grows replacements faster than it kills them. The Family Relations Council puts the overall toll of the war into this long-range perspective:

. . . in eight days, 40,000 males will be added to the population, or enough to match the number killed in Vietnam. Our population is so large that a temporary doubling of the death rate for one small segment will pass unnoticed by most people. Who does bear the impact most? Widows, bereaved children, parents, etc. We do not know at this time what proportion of servicemen have wives and children, but we can surmise from Veterans Administration data that 6,300 widows were added to the compensation rolls as a result of Vietnam deaths in the year beginning July, 1968. Then there are the unidentifiable women whose prospects for marriage are changed. Considering that the life expectancy of a man at 20 is 70, or 50 additional years, and the median age of the casualties is about 22, then 40,000 deaths translates into 2 million man-years of life lost. Since 95% of Americans can be expected to marry, this means that some high proportion of 2 million woman-years will be spent without a man. This is a large figure which also must be put in perspective: there are more widows than widowers at every age level, because death rates for men exceed those for women. In the U.S. in 1968 there were 9,305,000 widows and 2,142,000 widowers. Also, some 2,414,000 children had lost their fathers as of January 1966, from all causes.[2]

Even into the raw figures of death there come the elitist notions of the Selective Service System, with its insistence on the greater worth of men who serve the nation best. Under a recent amendment to the regulations governing Dependency and Indemnity Compensation, the national state has set the following sort of scale for lives lost in Vietnam: bereaved families of the lowest grade servicemen are given $167 per month per widow plus $20 per month per child. The widow of high grade officers are given $426 a month plus $20 per child. In short, the same sort of ranking of importance accorded the husbands in life is now passed along and accorded to the survivors after the death of the ranked subject. Perhaps this will channel the high ranking widows into more useful service to the state than could be expected from the low ranking widows. It is notable, of course, that the children are all ranked the same for purposes of indemnification. Their turn to be ranked comes later.

The Council on Family Relations, again, has studied how that ranking takes place and their report "Differential Impact on the Negro Minority"[3] is worth quoting at length. The points it makes cannot be said any more starkly.

An extensive study would be required to determine how representative of all U.S. families are the bereaved families. We do have information on Selective Service practices which suggest that the Negro minority is bearing significantly more than its share of the death and liability, not just of young men in general, but of those young men who, among Negroes represent the upper echelon of achievement and potential.*

---

* Fact Sheet on Negroes in the Armed Forces, Department of Defense (annually since 1966).

In view of the furor stirred up by the Moynihan report on the Negro family, and the Jensen family of genetic factors in intelligence, we have a responsibility to examine any policies which contribute to the systematic or disproportionate weakening of any ethnic group. Genasthenia may be a useful term for such weakening, in this instance by selecting the "better" half of a population group for increased risk of death and disability.

In 1967–8 about 7% of white draftees failed mental tests (measuring educational level, mainly) as compared with 27% of Negroes. On the other hand when it came to the medical examination, over 30% of the whites were disqualified, as against 16–20% of the Negroes. This would imply that Negroes have lower educational levels than whites (true) but that whites have more medical ailments (false: the statistics should be reversed in the induction centers, since disabling conditions and related ailments run higher— perhaps 75% higher—in young Negro men). The discrepancy must be due to discrimination in the amount and quality of medical care, if not in the Selective Service examination itself. Selective Service data showing medical disqualifications by state confirms this: Mississippi disqualifies few, Massachusetts many—of both races, but always favoring whites.

In sum, the more privileged white tends to be excused from service, either by deferment, or, in many cases, medical disqualification. The better-off black—high school graduate, no gross handicaps—is likely to serve.

It appears that inductees represent an American underclass. Negro young men already are an underclass, so all but the tiny upper crust are likely to be drafted and exposed to the ultimate risk. It is true that military service has also been a channel of advancement for many underprivileged Americans. But at what cost to the Negro minority and to the nation? This question is forced on us by Vietnam, where 13% of the deaths are Negroes—a total of 4,000 so far— although they number only 9% of servicemen.

The immediate issue is not whether the factors in Negro advancement are genetic or social, both, etc., but whether disadvantaged men who have attained relative social success are being selectively eliminated from the social and genetic pool of their ethnic group and their country.

How the Selective Service System begins from a bias that makes this "genasthenia" a natural development is indicated by the makeup of the boards themselves and then by the actions of those who make them up. The Report of the National Advisory Commission on selective service operations shows the anatomy of the boards thoroughly and a remarkable doctoral dissertation completed in 1968 by G. L. Wamsley[4] has shown how that anatomy acts.

First, nearly three-fourths of all members of Selective Service System boards, those "neighbors" to which the literature of the System fondly refers, are in white-collar occupations and a stunning 98.5 percent of the members of those boards also are white in color as well. Of 17,123 members of local Selective Service System boards, only 261 are black. It is striking to recall that in recent years, it has been possible to demand that even jury trials reflect some general ethnic representation but that in the selection of men possibly to be killed for the state, the black people who are killed proportionately more than others are represented by a board membership that is only a fraction of their percentage of the total population. (There are about 150 board members who are Puerto Rican and about the same number of Spanish-Americans. There are only thirty-some Oriental board members and, at last count, only sixteen American Indian board members.)

Another doctoral dissertation, by Donald Dean Stewart, drives directly to the sort of thinking that the middle-class board members bring with them.

There was an observed tendency among board members

to refer to the standards of middle class behavior in decisions . . . irregular work records, arrests, drunkenness,
petty offenses were felt to be "better off in the Army." Mari-
tal unions not sanctioned by law were disregarded in classification, even if it was of long standing and involved children.[5]

A striking example of this in action is shown in an
observation reported in the Wamsley dissertation. It involved a registrant who wanted a critical occupation deferment to continue work with the YMCA.

The registrant had all the qualities that board members
viewed positively. He was pleasant, clean-cut, well-dressed,
forthright, and confident but with respectful demeanor. Such
characteristics were always looked upon as "presenting one-
self well." During the interview the subject of social class
was brought up.
Chairman: What—a—sort of people do you try to reach with
your clubs—are these the—a—lower classes—er—poor—
Registrant: (Hesitantly) Well—a—no, they're just middle
class kids in the suburban high school. They're all basically
good kids, but we feel they need a program like this.[6]

The Board voted for deferment. When the researcher
expressed his surprise to the clerk the next day, she admitted that the decision had surprised her too.

Well, I think they liked his personality. He sold himself
well and I think mostly they thought he was doing some good
work. That boy knew what he wanted to do. He wasn't
just killing time like so many others. He'd turned down all
those other jobs that offered more money and they probably felt that he was doing the community a real service in
the long run. Don't you think he is? I mean, seeing those
kids get into something worthwhile instead of becoming de-
linquents or something like that.[7]

Besides the distinct class consciousness that has shown itself in all studies of the boards, there is a pro-state bias as well, a bias toward the warfare state. Some sixty-seven percent of board members are themselves veterans of military service. Even the ones who are not veterans overwhelmingly represent those class interests most distinctly served by the state and its defenses. Also, of the military veterans on the boards, a heavy percentage are either members of or were actually selected for their jobs by various veterans' organizations. Those organizations, in turn, have distinct warfare-state interests. Gabriel Almond's book, *The American People and Foreign Policy,* sums up that interest.

> The veterans' organizations in the United States have historically placed special emphasis on a strong national defense policy. Their general ideology has been nationalist and patriotic, and they have led in efforts to suppress subversive elements. As an aspect of their nationalism they have shown strong distrust of foreigners, and they have advocated the restriction of immigration.[8]

Wamsley, in his study, reported that it became "evident that Almond has caught some of the main elements of the outlook of board members." [9] In particular, the Selective Service System has what Wamsley calls "close ties" to the American Legion and the Veterans of Foreign Wars. He cites states where the selection of boards was entirely from lists prepared by the veterans' organizations. Also cited is the almost reflexive action of classifying alien residents as I-A because "board members claimed that aliens were here to avoid the draft in their own countries" (even in cases where their country had no draft).[10]

As to the attitude towards subversives, with its inevitable consequences for the young men who come to their boards with long hair or any radical characteristics at all, Wamsley reports that after the meetings of boards he and others observed that "conversations easily turned" to subversives.

> There were discussions covering such matters as: the mistake of disarming after World War II: how General Marshall had "given away China"; MacArthur had the "right idea"; how America was being "suckered into all that foreign aid"; and how "the only thing those Russians and Chinese understand is muscle." [11]

To these same board members also, of course, falls the on-the-spot job of carrying into action the channeling motivation of the Selective Service System's overview. In practice, what this means is that the pall of fear that conscription casts is left to do the job pretty much on its own—simply frightening people into work that they vaguely hope will get them off rather than, on the basis of objective information, pushing them there.

The fact of the matter, as close observation of board activities shows, is that the board members have little actual information on which to base any idea at all of the so-called national interest. They act solely on the basis of their own class interest. And knowing what that class interest is, overwhelmingly middle-class and property-centered, the channeling operation becomes not some vague national interest at all, but very specifically a class interest. And that, in turn, simply adds up to the fact that the national interest, with all the patriotic window-dressing discarded, is, after all, a class interest, the interest of the propertied class.

Wamsley describes the dynamics of the national-class interest.

> Board members were constantly torn between trying to operationalize the impossibly vague criterion of national interest and adaptation of processes to the individual situation.

Because they were expected to operationalize some nebulous national manpower policy, they tried to act on the basis of national health, safety, or interest and to treat similar cases in a uniform manner; but at the same time, they felt driven to adjust the processes of Selective Service to individuals. Because they lacked informational resources to do either, they reacted in a disturbingly large portion of cases by treating registrants in accordance with the relationships they developed with them in the interview or from letters in the files. Consequently, the seemingly insignificant things like posture and dress, wording of letters, and who signed them seemed to become inordinately important in decisions.[12]

Typical queries used by the board members to arrive at their decisions as to the national interest are listed by Wamsley as:

"What do you do with your spare time?"
"You don't like to submit to authority, do you?"
"What kind of car do you drive?"
"Were you ever in the Boy Scouts?"
"Where do you do your loafing?"
"Does your father have a problem with drinking or anything?" [13]

Wamsley's striking conclusion about the final attitude of the boards toward the people who are their merchandise is that

members feel a concern about equity for each individual is unrealistic and unnecessary to achieve acceptance. This means that unintentionally the articulate and higher strata registrants are the recipients of such concern for equity as the System can afford to dispense.[14]

Ironically, the clear class bias of the Selective Service System has not worked to weaken its acceptance in the society but has, instead, served to strengthen it. The reason is that, as a study by Karen Oppenheim[15] has shown, the lower the educational level of persons sampled, the higher the percentage that thought the draft was fair. The people severely impacted by the draft, in other words, do not seem to see it as a class abuse or oppression.

Clearly, one of the reasons must lie in where they get what education they do get. They get it in state schools, schools whose curricula admittedly are designed in the lower grades to produce well-adjusted citizens and not simply educated humans. The more one must depend upon the official state mythmakers, and be in a class position where survival, if not sanity, depends on knowing one's place, the more the burden of the draft is likely to be seen as simply one more of those hardships which providence has chosen, in its inscrutable wisdom, to visit upon the poor. It is only in very recent years that the idea has begun to occur that being poor in the first place might be the magnet that attracts those hardships in a disproportionate amount. Adding to the irony, given our descriptions of local Selective Service System boards, it is probable that a young man who went before a board with such an idea in mind would probably be marked as the first to go. Inexorably in that way, too, the system is a class defense.

One other possibility has been advanced to explain the willingness of those who are treated most unfairly by local boards to think that, in fact, they are being treated properly. That reason is the hope that through military service they might be able to achieve the training and the opportunities which were not available to them as ordinary citizens. Even so, one would not expect that conscription would be the only way to get them if, indeed, they are so eager to get ahead. Just how to classify a society in which men find a fair shot at self-development available only by risking their lives in political wars is a problem upon whose answer rests one of the essential descriptions of anyone's political position.

There is a final irony in the fact that much of the Selective Service System's acceptance is felt by public opinion samplers to be based upon the idea that the boards, because they are local, actually do represent the old-fashioned verities of localism, neighborhood, participation, and so forth. And, on paper and even rhetorically, that is true. The boards are local. But the goals are national. The leadership is national and paramilitary, and the ambience within which the boards function is the ambience of the total state (as embodied, for instance, in the channeling memo which was discussed in the previous chapter).

The fact of the matter is that the Selective Service System for all of its quaint structure has fitted nicely into the new national neighborhood, the sort of place described politically by Samuel Beer in his "Liberalism and the National Idea."

> The National Idea is not only a view of American federalism, but also a principle of public policy. As a principle of public policy, it is a doctrine of what today is commonly called "nation building." Its imperative is to use the power of the nation as a whole not only to promote social improvement and individual excellence, but also to make the nation more solidary [*sic*], more cohesive, more independent in its growing diversity: in short to make the nation more of a nation.[16]

That the Selective Service System, for all of its local structure, serves that nationalizing policy consciously has been apparent for years, even before the channeling memo was written. As far back as 1952, for instance, in a book entitled *Student Deferment in Selective Service,* M. H. Trytten wrote:

We are rebuilding our strength from the low point result-
ing from our precipitate demobilization of 1946 and 1947.
This means we are operating our research, development, and
production facilities under extreme pressure for speed. Not
only must we design and produce a stockpile of weapons
adequate to meet a possible military crisis, but we must also
carry on activities essential to maintaining our civilization
and its program.[17]

It is obvious that in this context, the Selective Service
System and the state ownership of citizens that it represents
is the vital framework in which civilization must be defined.

One significant question left open by the wide acceptance
of the Selective Service frame of mind is one of tactical
significance and not strategic implication, whether or how
long the state's utilization of its manpower, the citizens,
will be operated on the limited, directed-choice basis of the
Selective Service sort as contrasted with a shift to a more
overt, total approach such as national service. That this
question could remain pertinent even after a shift to a
voluntary *military* system is indicated by this description of
national service written by a professional apologist for the
concept, Donald J. Eberly, editor of "National Service,"
and executive director of the National Service Secretariat.

Just as vital to the national service concept . . . is its
independence of the Selective Service System. For if a national service program were dependent for its existence on
the military draft and if in time there was no longer a need
for the draft, it would mean the end of national service, or an
unneeded conscription.

What counts, therefore, is the frame of mind—a frame
of mind that is not substantially changed just by changes
in military manpower procurement but which is conditioned
above all by a view of the nation and the place of the

citizen within that nation or, as the entire state philosophy now would have it, the place of the citizen under that nation.

NOTES

1. "Effects of U.S. Casualties in Vietnam on American Families," National Council on Family Relations, 1969 Annual Meeting, Washington, D.C., Oct. 22–25, 1969, pp. 1–2.
2. *Ibid.,* p. 2.
3. *Ibid.,* pp. 4–5.
4. G. L. Wamsley, "Selective Service and American Political Culture," Ph.D. Dissertation, University of Pittsburgh, 1968.
5. Donald Dean Stewart, "Local Board, A Study of the Place of Volunteer Participation in a Bureaucratic Organization," (unpublished Ph.D. Dissertation, Columbia University, 1950), p. 150.
6. Wamsley, *op. cit.,* p. 277.
7. *Ibid.*
8. Gabriel Almond, *The American People and Foreign Policy* (New York: Frederick A. Praeger, 1966), pp. 171–174.
9. Wamsley, *op. cit.,* p. 280.
10. *Ibid.,* p. 281.
11. *Ibid.,* p. 282.
12. *Ibid.,* p. 287–288.
13. *Ibid.,* p. 293.
14. *Ibid.,* p. 334.
15. Karen Oppenheim, "Attitudes of Younger American Men Toward Selective Service," National Opinion Research Center, University of Chicago, March 1966, p. 15.
16. Samuel Beer, "Liberalism and the National Idea," *Public Interest* No. 5, (Fall 1966), p. 71.
17. M. H. Trytten, *Student Deferment in Selective Service* (Minneapolis: University of Minnesota, 1952), p. 26.
18. Donald J. Eberly, "National Needs and National Service," *Current History,* August 1968, p. 71.

Chapter 6

The Course
of Control

If the Selective Service System, in all of its ramifications, may be said to have effectively furthered the national interest, it also has been accused of being used as an effective barrier against those who wish to change the direction of that national interest. Specifically, it has been charged by the Southern Conference Educational Fund that "increasingly, the work of young, effective organizers is being curtailed" because of the draft.

Evidently, organizing to improve people's conditions is considered neither "necessary" nor "in the national interest."

SCEF, in turn, is accused by various agencies of the state of being dangerously radical for wanting to improve people's conditions in the first place.

Two southern workers in the American radical movement are cited as prime examples of how the SSS is used to fight social change even while advancing the status quo of the national state's interests.[1] One is Joe Mulloy, twenty-five, raised in Louisville in a working-class family, in which the father was a plumber and a minor union official. While at the University of Kentucky in 1964 Mulloy started working with a student group called Appalachian Volunteers that was involved with poor people in the hills of the region. At one point the group applied for and was given a federal grant and Mulloy was able to join the group on a full-time staff basis. The program in which he was involved brought student volunteers and VISTA workers into contact and into work-sharing experiences with the mountain people. Whatever its worth, however, the program was viewed increasingly by Mulloy and some others as concentrating more on providing experience in such contact for the student volunteers, rather than actually concentrating on the solution of problems faced by the mountain people themselves.

Strip mining was one such problem. In such mining, and its related variant, auger mining, coal seams are exposed by cutting across the tops and around the sides of hills. Great quantities of earth, rocks, trees are moved in the process and represent a continuing source of slide damage to nearby homes as well as being sources of pollution. Mine owners are not, however, held liable for damage caused by such operations and, further, the mines pay only token taxes. Thus, booming in the midst of some of the nation's worst pockets of poverty, is one of its multi-billion businesses.

From the volunteer group with which he had been involved, Mulloy and some others moved to form local groups which would oppose strip mining, advocate coal taxation and, in effect, seek to put more and more of the natural resources of the area into the control of and into the service of the people of the area.

One result of the organizing work was a confrontation in which a homeowner actually faced down a bulldozer that was about to clear some mining land above his home. His neighbors were there to back him up, as was Mulloy and his wife. After a month-long continuation of this human wall against the bulldozer, the governor ordered a halt to that particular mining operation. It was a clear victory for a technique which could have spread rapidly.

Eleven days after the confrontation had succeeded, Mulloy was arrested and, with some others, was charged with sedition. The leader of the party that raided Mulloy's home and made the arrest was the founder of the Coal Operators' Association, then serving as State's Attorney. One month later the sedition law under which Mulloy was charged was found unconstitutional. And, at that point, the draft law took over. During the time of the hillside confrontation Mulloy had been ordered to report for induction. His status was that he was then appealing his reclassification, several months before, from an occupational deferment to I-A. He was able to get the induction order cancelled. But, two weeks after the sedition arrest, his appeal was unanimously denied and he was classified I-A. On the day after the sedition law was thrown out, Mulloy was ordered to report for induction, despite the fact that he was then out on bail pending a possible appeal by the state.

Convinced that the war in which he was about to be forced to serve was wrong and that he could not participate in it for moral reasons, he filed for status as a Conscientious Objector. The appeal was turned down. A new induction order was issued. Mulloy refused to step forward to accept induction and was convicted, for that refusal, in a federal court. At his trial, the clerk of his local board claimed that not once in seventeen years had the board exempted anyone from service as a CO. (It was the same board that refused to exempt Muhammad Ali as a Muslim minister.)

Of crucial interest is the fact that Mulloy's Selective Service file was shown to contain a full array of clippings and reports about his work as an organizer in the mountains and about his confrontation with the coal operators. The timing of his troubles with the System, the nature of the bias already shown by all studies of the System, the repeated philosophizing about the national interest, all clearly show the SSS expanding the concept of channeling from just putting people where they belong to stopping them from being where they shouldn't—such as out in the hills fighting for social justice.

More than six years later, the Supreme Court finally vindicated Mulloy by reversing a Court of Appeals decision. The Supreme Court ruling was important not only for Mulloy but also for many others across the country, because it made compulsory the reopening of draft cases by local boards and because it dealt definitively with the matter of use of the draft as an instrument of political repression.

Walter Collins, a Louisianan and a worker with the Student Nonviolent Coordinating Committee, SNCC, was involved in another case. After the full course of activism, beginning with the early sit-ins, he went on to work in the ambitious voter registration drives of Mississippi Summer in 1964. At Louisiana State in 1965–66 he not only continued to work on voter drives but became active in the movement against the war in Vietnam. In particular he began to compile exact casualty lists for the black sections of New Orleans, issuing pamphlets to show how many more blacks than whites were being killed to, as he put it, "fight for other people's freedom thousands of miles away, when they were not free themselves." There was considerable objection to his pamphleteering and, among other things, the local newspapers stopped printing pictures of war dead, thus visually blunting the point that Collins kept making. Meanwhile, his mother, Virginia Collins, also was active in organizing among the poor and in antiwar work, and became a regional vice-president of the Republic of New Africa, a separatist group.

Collins' problems with the draft grew immediately after the New Orleans trouble with his antiwar work. He had, at the time, moved to the University of Michigan where he was a full-time graduate student. In January 1967, six months before the ruling went into effect which disallowed graduate deferments, Collins was classified I-A. He wrote his New Orleans draft board, asking to appeal the apparently arbitrary withdrawal of his student deferment. The letter, it was subsequently claimed by the draft board, never reached them. In June he was ordered to report for a physical. He then formally asked to meet with the board to discuss his status and went to New Orleans to do so. There he was told that he would have to write another letter and await the board's regular meeting. When he returned to Michigan there was an induction order waiting for him, issued even before his visit to the board. The date for induction had, by then, gone by—in a time period during which he actually had been at the draft board involved. Flying back to New Orleans he was told, in effect, that there was nothing he could do about it except go for induction. He went twice. And twice he was told to leave the induction center because he was wearing antiwar buttons. At a subsequent visit to the induction center he was examined by a medical officer who taunted him in a racist way. Then he was told to sit in an office and wait. After three hours, he got up and left without hindrance. By then he had determined to simply refuse induction. He moved to New York, went to work in the peace movement there and was arrested—and convicted of five counts of refusing induction for which he drew maximum sentences totaling twenty-five years.

The foreman of the jury was a man who had said, "I'm a spy, a secret agent for the Army. Would that prejudice the case?" Also selected as jurors were several women who were the wives or mothers of policemen. It was, in fact, a jury that would have been comfortable with their peers on local draft boards who also had come in all probability from similar situations and arrived with similar dispositions toward men like Walter Collins. Despite recent orders which have told local boards that they must not punish dissenters by application of the power to induct—as though a regulation can somehow change a process that is by this time virtually acculturated—the underlying fact is that the raw power used by the Selective Service System in the service of the state is a power that has been thoroughly legalized by the highest court in the land. It is a power, further, that the court has countenanced using in the past in cases remarkably similar to those in which, today, dissidents are silenced under the canons of conscription.

One of the most famed of all conscription cases involved a clearly political issue. That is the case of Eugene V. Debs, head of the Socialist Party during the First World War. The crime involved was a speech, delivered by Debs, mainly about socialism. In that speech, he spoke of the fight for socialism as similar to the fight against the war which, he said, was being waged by capitalists against capitalists and for capitalists. He did, at that point, endorse an antiwar statement which recommended active opposition to the war, mass demonstrations, petitions and so forth.

He was arrested, tried, and convicted and the conviction was upheld by the Supreme Court unanimously. Writing that opinion for the Court, Justice Oliver Wendell Holmes pointed out that the jury

> could not find the defendant guilty for advocacy of any of his opinions unless the words had as their natural tendency and reasonably probable effect to obstruct the recruiting service, etc. and unless the defendant had the specific intent to do so in mind.[2]

Earlier, Holmes had issued one of his most famous legal dicta in a similar case. It involved Charles Schenck, a vigorous advocate of disobeying the conscription laws. It was in upholding a conviction of Schenck that Holmes promulgated his "clear and present danger" doctrine, saying that

> The question in every case is whether the words used are used in such circumstances and are of such a nature as to create a clear and present danger that they will bring about the substantive evils that Congress has a right to prevent.[3]

The clear and present danger, of course, was a clear and present danger to the state itself and to its crucial power to control citizens. Then it was the control of those citizens during a time of declared national emergency. Since then it has become more and more clearly a power to control them at all times "in the national interest" as the SSS's own vision of its role in society has shown.

When the cases of the First World War were being decided, there had not developed as clear a notion as now of the uses of indirection in controlling the people, so that there was some discussion about the possibility of drafting workers directly for service in defense industries. A nice point of political or social morality was made at the time. It would not be proper, it was said, to draft men to labor for factory owners who were doing handsomely on war profits. In an early or crude version of the later SSS channeling procedures, the War Department at that time simply issued a "work or fight" order and the lines lengthened at the employment offices of the profitable war industries.

By 1940, however, in a case involving a challenge to a draft board, the Supreme Court had decided that "work or fight" was too confining and that actual fighting should not be considered a requisite of putting into action the state's awesome power to control its citizens. Justice Hugo Black, at that time, wrote:

> When the Selective Service and Training Act was passed in September, 1940, most of the world was at war. The preamble of the act declared it was "imperative to increase and train the personnel of the armed forces of the United States." The danger of attack by our present enemies, if not imminent, was real, as subsequent events have grimly demonstrated. The Congress was faced with the urgent necessity of integrating all the nation's people and forces for national defense. That dire consequences might flow from apathy and delay was well understood. Accordingly the Act was passed to mobilize national manpower with the speed which that necessity and understanding required.[4]

All that was needed from then on was a threat. The arbiters of that threat could only be the leaders of the state, now become the total leaders of the people.

The problem of mobilizing manpower and production on the factory battlefront was not as easily settled. Granting of industrial exemptions solved part of the problem, of course. Price and wage controls solved another part. Renegotiable contracts solved still another part. Significantly, in addition, however, incentive rewards also were employed. In short, and as usual, property was treated with the deepest respect, lives with the least. Curiously enough, in another Supreme Court decision, in 1948, the Court actually commented on the virtue of resisting the sort of controls for property that it, in all of its other decisions, had fully accepted in relation to people.

> Faced with this ironical alternative of converting the nation in effect into a totalitarian state in order to preserve itself from totalitarian domination, that alternative was steadfastly rejected.[5]

The rejection, of course, was for the alternatives as they applied to business, not to people generally. The decision swept away in that sentence any connection that others might have made between the totalitarian control of individuals and the totalitarian domination that was said to be so repugnant. Of sole concern was the resistance of controls over industry. The Supreme Court, notably, accepted the notion that it was in this area and not in the area of a conscriptable citizenry that the difference between the totalitarianism we were fighting and the totalitarianism we supposedly were resisting at home could be found.

From the end of the Second World War, and building upon the base of the Supreme Court's full acceptance of the idea of service to the national state, the concept of the cold, or perpetual even if peaceful, war extended the idea of control into the indefinite future, fighting or no fighting.

Stemming from the control-idea is the entire gathering of implications derived from the state's primary right to violate all of the rights of its citizens in order to protect the rights of the state. As one commentator on the Court's decision put it:

> The powers of Congress to require military service for the common defense are broad and far-reaching, for while the Constitution protects against invasions of individual rights, it is not a suicide pact.[6]

The suicide to be avoided is specifically not that of individuals but of the state and the interests which it actually does protect while violating the interests of individuals. The same attitude prevails through all of the Court's decisions and, indeed, throughout the official culture of the national state. If death, then let it be the death of the citizens. The state must not perish, even to save those lives.

Today, even should the Selective Service System end, as it well might, the problem of its heritage, a heritage written in all those years of establishing state preeminence, would persist. Already, prosecutions against political dissenters which once might have depended, as in the Debs or, later, Dr. Spock cases, upon resistance to conscription, are beginning to shift to other areas in which the right of the state to protect itself against the intent of words and speakers is rooted simply, like the Selective Service System itself, in that catch-all abstraction, the national interest.

It is less and less, today, the problem of making manpower available at chosen spots. It is more and more a question of closing out that manpower which has radical or resistance notions. The enemy, in this latest extension of the cold war, already has become, in the speeches of the Vice President as well as the Attorney General, not some distant enemy for which we need soldiers, but an internal enemy for which we need policemen. And the policemen, in turn, are often recruited directly from the armed forces which, adopting their own in-house version of SSS channeling, now encourage men to enroll in what might be called the civilian soldiery by permitting them early release from the martial soldiery.

The question that haunts our time is whether a justice of the Supreme Court in years hence might still be able to write that line about not "converting the nation in effect into a totalitarian state in order to preserve itself from totalitarian domination." Or is it already years too late? Conscription always has involved the question of just such domination. It has always been the entering wedge of that domination not by some alien threat but by the holders of power right here and right now.

NOTES

1. The entire male staff of SCEF has been harassed by Selective Service. For a sampling of numerous other cases, *see* Staughton Lynd, *We Won't Go* (Boston: Beacon Press, 1969).
2. Debs v. United States, 249 U.S. 211, 216 (1919).
3. Schenck v. United States, 249 U.S. 47 (1919).
4. Falbo v. United States, 320 U.S. 549, 551–552 (1944).
5. Lichter v. United States, 334 U.S. 742, 766 (1948).
6. Carl Brent Swisher, "The Supreme Court and Conscription," *Current History*, June 1968, p. 351.

Chapter 7

The Draft
and Public Policy

Patrick Henry said at the Virginia Ratifying Convention, "If your American chief be a man of ambition and abilities, how easy is it for him to render himself absolute! The army is in his hands. . . . Can he not, at the head of his army, beat down every opposition?" [1] Most of the American presidents have been ambitious, but few have been terribly able. Those who *were* both did much to extend the powers of the executive over those of the other branches of government. This has been especially true in that dangerous area of powers of war—the president as commander-in-chief.

The Constitution explicitly centralized far more military power in the president than had been the case in England or the individual colonies. Following the English example, however, Congress was given the important control of purse strings—with a requirement that military budgets be no more than two years in duration. In many ways, as

Charles Evans Hughes once remarked, the Constitution is a fighting document. Fresh from their experience of a weak executive and a vacillating legislature under the Articles of the Confederation, the constitutional signatories determined to have a strong central government under a popular head. Their concept was of a strong federal executive with strong state executives as well—and their president was to be above parties, elected by popular electors. The Civil War, modern communications and demands for an efficient welfare state, all made inroads into the power of the states. The needs of modern warfare, and particularly federal conscription of men, completed the construction of a powerful federal government and weak states.

Another trend developed to make the president the captive of large party organizations, which were responsive to specific regional and interest leaderships rather than to the people. With only two similar parties to choose from, each claiming to represent all Americans, and each really more interested in capturing a powerful bureaucracy with its patronage and contracts, the American people no longer have an important role in choosing the president. He has become almost entirely dependent upon party politicians and his own military and security—civilian bureaucrats, more and more isolated from public opinion. The antiwar and antidraft movements have partially reversed that trend by their demonstrations aimed at the presidency, but so far the primary reactions have been oriented to public relations rather than to program change. An end to the draft would be an important exception, and a precedent.

World War II saw the greatest increase in the powers of the president in our history, particularly of his war-related powers. It was in the heat of that war that the only substantive ruling by the Supreme Court was given on the constitutionality of conscription. It is well-known that Woodrow

Wilson feared our involvement in World War I chiefly because of what it would do to the nation at home in restricting freedoms and building a centralized state power. Even after he took the dreaded steps into war and a draft, he refused to be characterized as commander-in-chief. Franklin Roosevelt felt few such qualms. At one point he demanded new powers from Congress and asserted that he would take them anyway if necessary. The great corporations, instead of defying this increase in national power over the economy, determined to get as much of the action for themselves as possible. It was their leadership which urged a continuation of the close cooperation of government and business with the military after the war. They had managed, during wartime, to quell the rising labor consciousness, and the labor movement emerged from the war as a tame partner in the new consensus coalition. No president could have been better suited for this steady growth of the federal executive than FDR, champion of the people in the New Deal. Mr. Roosevelt made sweeping claims for presidential power:

> In the event that the Congress should fail to act, and act adequately, I shall accept the responsibility and I will act. . . . The President has the power, under the Constitution and under Congressional Acts, to take measures necessary to avert a disaster which would interfere with the winning of the war. . . . I cannot tell what powers may have to be exercised in order to win this war.[2]

Nowhere has the power and activity of the president been more greatly extended than in his ability, based on technical military advice often secret and unavailable for Congressional scrutiny, to commit American troops abroad and to declare emergency rules at home in the name of "national defense." When the president decides national security is at stake, it would seem there is little argument possible. In Laos, the Congo, Lebanon, South Vietnam and elsewhere around the world, the presidents since World War II have increasingly sent American "advisors," machinery and troops without Congressional approval or even knowledge. A particularly dangerous result of the increase in executive power has been that policy has shifted away from public and private groups to secret or well-hidden organs of the federal bureaucracy—both military and civilian. The commitment of manpower abroad or the federal intervention in strikes at home have been carried out by the president in the name of "national security." There was virtually no opposition until the Senate Foreign Relations Committee hearings on Vietnam and Laos began in 1968.

Only once was an extension of executive power repudiated—and that was by the Supreme Court, not by Congress. President Truman had seized the steel mills in order to get them going again (rather than invoke the provisions of the Taft-Hartley Act against Democratic labor). The Supreme Court rejected this action. Justice Robert H. Jackson wrote:

> Nothing in our Constitution is plainer than that a declaration of war is entrusted only to Congress. . . . no doctrine that the Court could promulgate would seem to me more sinister and alarming than that a President whose conduct of foreign affairs is so largely uncontrolled, and often even is unknown, can vastly enlarge his mastery over the internal affairs of the country by his own commitment of the Nation's armed forces to some foreign venture.[3]

The seizure of the steel mills was struck down, but injunctions against strikes were not, nor even the power of the president to send troops abroad without Congressional approval. Never was the draft challenged, despite its obvious violation of the Constitution in giving the president war-making powers in peacetime. A recent book on U.S. war policy includes this interchange in the steel mill controversy between the court and the Assistant Attorney General, Holmes Baldridge:

> THE COURT: So you contend the Executive has unlimited power in time of emergency?
>
> MR. BALDRIDGE: He has the power to take such action as is necessary to meet the emergency.
>
> THE COURT: If the emergency is great, it is unlimited is it?
>
> MR. BALDRIDGE: I suppose if you carry it to its logical conclusion, that is true.[4]

The dangers of such an assumption were outlined long before by a young Congressman, Abraham Lincoln, reacting to the way in which President Polk had involved the United States in Mexico:

> Allow the President to invade a neighboring nation, whenever *he* shall deem it necessary . . . and you allow him to do so, *whenever he may choose to say* he deems it necessary . . . and you allow him to make war at pleasure. . . . Kings had always been involving and impoverishing their people in wars, pretending generally, if not always, that the good of the people was the object. This our Convention understood to be the most oppressive of all kingly oppressions; and they resolved so to frame the Constitution that *no one man* should hold the power of bringing this oppression upon us. [Italics in original.] [5]

A U.S. State Department document, "The Legality of U.S. Participation in the Defense of Viet-Nam," counters this claim by Lincoln, and asserts overwhelming powers for the president:

> Under the Constitution, the President, in addition to being Chief Executive, is Commander in Chief of the Army and Navy. . . .

These duties carry very broad powers, including the power to deploy American forces abroad and commit them to military operations when the President deems such action necessary to maintain the security and defense of the United States. . . .

In 1787 the world was a far larger place, and the framers probably had in mind attacks upon the United States. In the 20th century, the world has grown much smaller. An attack on a country far from our shores can impinge directly on the nation's security. . . . If he [the President] considers that deployment of U.S. forces to South Viet-Nam is required . . . he is constitutionally empowered to take those measures.[6]

The executive, through its military operations and the pronouncements of its foreign policy experts, now holds almost unlimited power. At a time when our military was small and limited to defense, the executive provided a civilian check on possible military adventurism or militarism. Today, the executive is *primarily* the director of a huge civilian-military complex dedicated to making war whenever "national interest" is deemed at stake by that same executive. As John Foster Dulles once remarked when asked about a particular clandestine American involvement in Indonesia, "Our interest is where we say it is." In this process, not only has the Congress lost its war and peace powers, but the people have been excluded by experts and their secrecy from any direct participation or even proper knowledge of American foreign policy. The distinction between civilian and military has been wiped out, and to call for civilian control over the military is only to ask for more of the same: increased executive power. Where would be the merit in "civilian control" if the president directed the military to dismiss Congress because its debate damaged "national security"?

A major role in this rise of executive power has been

played by the "peacetime" draft. With the constant assurance of a free labor supply in draftees—and unlimited in number—the president can effectively get around the Constitutional provision for bi-yearly checks on military expenditures. He can also escalate American involvement abroad or initiate new interventions without asking Congress—or even making a major public announcement about the increase. This is not only true of minor and short-term crises, but much more the case in slow and practically permanent involvements. The draft was used to provide security for our intervention in the Congo, both before and after our policy was announced. It was a major tool of the president's in initiating and then in sustaining the build-up in Vietnam. Without the draft, he would have needed to go to Congress to clearly state the goals, asking either for a draft or for greatly increased appropriations for more soldiers. That would have allowed public and Congressional debate before the major commitment in Vietnam, instead of the hollow Tonkin Resolution after the fact.

It is especially interesting to compare the importance (or unimportance) of the draft in two cases: the Cuba missile crisis and the Berlin Wall crisis. The chart shows that the missile crisis was in fact completely an atomic bluff—or rather, that it did not involve preparations for war, invasion or defense at any level other than our commitment to total nuclear warfare. The Berlin Wall "crisis," on the other hand, was clearly of another sort.

Increasing pressure had mounted during 1960 and 1961 for an end to American troop occupation in Germany and a settlement along the lines of the one in Austria. Such a "German solution" was favored neither by the USSR nor by the U.S. The Soviets felt the need of maintaining troops in East Germany, since the rejection of the Rapacki plan meant it would be impossible to neutralize West Germany.

On the other hand, American economic involvement and the political importance of our military presence in West Germany were so great that the United States did not look favorably on developments that would change the German status quo. When Kennedy met Khrushchev in Vienna in the early summer of 1961, the Soviet leader made clear to Kennedy the need to close off the hole in East German security. Early in August, Senator Fulbright, then spokesman for the administration on foreign policy, remarked on a national television program that he would not be surprised if the East Germans were forced to build a wall. This was before any public discussion by the East Germans of that possibility.

The evidence now indicates that America was well informed on the possibilities of Berlin wall-building, and that we had given tacit consent for it. The building of the wall was meant, from the Soviet point of view, to calm the east-west crisis, not to provoke a new one. The American reaction was loud, but without any significant attempt to intervene—a fact which almost cost the American protégé Adenauer his election that year. Johnson and Kennedy later made a great show of protesting the inhumanity of the wall, and Kennedy promised eternal protection of West Berlin with his famous *"Ich bin ein Berliner."* Yet the crisis cooled with great speed, and in fact the total division of Berlin has created a far less volatile situation there—so much so that the Berlin government complained in the late sixties of neglect and lack of interest from Bonn. In order to use this "crisis" as a political and military basis for continued vigilance in Europe and as evidence of America's continued hard line against any Communist "aggression," the draft was used by the president both before and after the Wall went up. Quite suddenly in July, Kennedy announced the doubling of draft calls for August, and even before the

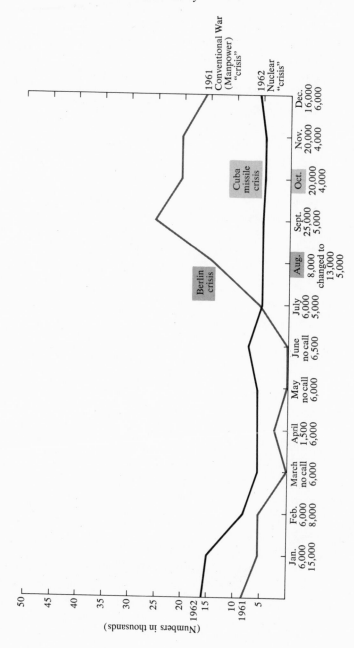

Source: New York Times News Index

Fielding M. McGehee
NCRD—March 1970

Wall in August, he set the September call at its highest level since the Korean War. Although seeking authority to call up massive reserves and National Guard, Kennedy avoided political controversy by raising draft quotas instead. Since no one outside the administration was really informed on the nature of the "crisis" or about the tacit understanding to allow the building of a wall while maintaining West Berlin intact, the reasons for increased draft calls were difficult to understand. They were not debated in Congress. As former President Eisenhower said in his call for bipartisan support, "If he increases the draft quota, he must be doing it for a good reason." [7]

It is this trust in the judgment of one man, insulated from controversial or contrary notions by an efficient corps of military and civilian experts, that must be questioned if freedom and democracy are again to take precedence over false concepts of security. The military draft is an extraordinary war power in the hands of the president. It has led to an increase in all his other war powers. The ease with which a military solution may be applied, because of the draft and its blank check for manpower, leads the nation into a preference for such military "solutions" even in areas where only political or economic solutions are called for. The availability of a large conscript army becomes tempting at home as well as abroad, and "military solutions" become popular even domestically. Such a development is wholly incompatible with freedom, yet it goes hand in hand with the tendency to avoid the desperate needs behind urban and ethnic unrest, and to resort to quick repressive measures.

As Vernon Dibble has said, manpower in the form of armament workers and drafted soldiers is warpower unchecked by popular pressures.[8] It is also the power of the state to coerce and fully control its citizens for state purposes. It is no accident that every major aggressive power since Napoleon has used the draft to forge its authority at home and fight its wars abroad. Nor is it an exaggeration to say that a nation's political and social health can be judged by the frequency of its resort to conscription. Practically every *coup d'état* in this century has occurred in conscripted armies with a professional officer corps.[9] Rather than civilizing the military, the draft reaches into every home to militarize the society. After their short terms, the draftees become the millions of well-trained veterans whose loyalty and zeal for military causes is well-known. After all, when one man is duped or coerced into a "service" which plays all kinds of havoc with his life, he is liable to be angry if others escape such problems. The draft has provided a military influence on public policy at home, an incentive for "military solutions" abroad, a way for the president to circumvent the Constitutional necessities of declaring war, and a precedent for thorough control of the citizens by the state. Merlo Pusey closes his book on the increasing powers of the president by declaring:

> It is time to bury the bizarre concept of inherent executive power to make war along with the divine right of kings and the super-race heresy that ravaged Europe a few decades ago.

> If Congress will not authorize a war, limited or full-fledged, after reasonably full knowledge of the facts and sober deliberations, the American people should not be in it. Our first and largest constitutional obligation . . . is to move toward restoration of that principle.[10]

The draft has been the handmaiden of increased executive authority and the motor for an acceptance of total state power never before possible in laissez-faire America. If we are to restore to the citizen his right of personal freedom, and if we are to restore to the people their right of consent and restraint on foreign policy and war, the draft must be abolished.

NOTES

1. Quoted in Ernest R. May, ed., *The Ultimate Decision* (New York: George Braziller, 1960), p. 5.

2. Quoted in Merle J. Pusey, *Big Government: Can We Control It?* (New York: Harper & Row, 1945), p. 50.

3. Youngstown Sheet & Tube Co. v. Sawyer, 343 U.S. 579 (1952).

4. Merle J. Pusey, *The Way We Go to War* (Boston: Houghton-Mifflin, 1969) pp. 157–58.

5. Abraham Lincoln, *The Collected Works of Abraham Lincoln,* ed. Roy P. Blaster et al., vols. (New Brunswick, N.J.: Rutgers University Press, 1953), 1:451–52.

6. Quoted in Pusey, *The Way We Go to War,* pp. 6–7.

7. *New York Times,* 23 July 1961, p. 1.

8. Vernon Dibble, "The Garrison Society," *Radical Perspectives on Social Problems* (Los Angeles: California State College, 1968), 271 ff.

9. See Edward Luttwak, *Coup d'Etat* (New York: Knopf, 1968).

10. Pusey, *Big Government,* p 190.

Chapter 8

The Cost of
Voluntary Defense*

The cost of the draft and the cost of ending the draft are quite different concepts. They are often confused, however, and require careful elucidation. In this chapter, we will demonstrate both that the draft is a very "costly" means of raising manpower, in comparison with a voluntary system, and that the budgetary cost of a volunteer force would most likely exceed that of the draft system. The key to this seeming paradox lies in the different definitions of cost used in each concept. In the former, the cost of providing a product or service is taken, in the economic

---

* The findings of this chapter on the economics of ending the draft are not central to the basic theoretical assumptions held elsewhere by the authors. Economics play a key role, however, in the politics of ending the draft, and this survey provides the latest and best data available. It was written by Stewart W. Kemp, a consulting economist for the President's Commission on an All-Volunteer Armed Force.

sense, as the best alternative use of the resources required to support that function. Thus the real cost of the draft is the difference in the amount of resources required by a draft over a voluntary system to provide an armed force of equally effective size. In the latter concept, however, cost is understood (in general casual usage) as increase in budgetary expense. Thus the cost of ending the draft is the increase in the budget required to sustain the same effective force level as a draft. In order to avoid further confusion, we will use the term "cost" only as defined by the economist: the best alternative use of the real resources involved. Where the second meaning is intended, we will refer to "budgetary expense."

The draft is a more costly and less efficient means of providing manpower than a volunteer force. Briefly, there are three reasons for the inefficiency of the draft: first, there is a net decline in real output because draftees' productivity in the civilian labor market exceeds that required to be a soldier; second, many draft-eligible men alter their lives to avoid induction; and third, the draft produces higher turnover and attendant training costs within the military itself. In order to understand how these effects are caused, it is helpful to look for a moment at the analytics of conscription as an economic institution. Conscription is essentially a tax. It is a hidden tax paid in kind; it is a levy which never appears in the budget, but is a tax nonetheless.

In providing any public service, a government faces two alternatives. On the one hand, it can expropriate the necessary labor and materials. On the other hand, it can buy them on the open market, using funds obtained through general taxation. The former method is called a tax-in-kind, since the payment is made in labor and resources. This method of taxation has been employed for centuries; in fact, it was the predominant form until the development of modern monetary systems enabled a more equal distribution of the tax burden. Such a system has never been popular in America. With the exception of occasional exercise of the right of eminent domain, the draft of the past thirty years stands as the only institutionalization of a tax-in-kind since ratification of the Constitution. This mode of taxation has been resented for three reasons: first, it tends to involve a substantial deprivation of liberty for those compelled to supply the required services; second, glaring inequities result, as only a few citizens pay the lion's share of the cost of the service which benefits all; third, a tax-in-kind which does not appear in the budget distorts social decision making by concealing the true cost of services.

The amount of tax paid by a reluctant serviceman is simply the difference between the prevailing rate of military compensation and that rate which would induce him to volunteer of his own free will. Thus a man who would volunteer if paid $8,000 per annum, but who receives only $2,100 per annum as a draftee, is paying an annual tax of $5,900, a rate of almost 75%. The amount of tax paid by an individual varies with his civilian opportunities and the extent of his preference or distaste for military service. Since military pay for draftees is constant, both the amount and the rate of the tax increase with civilian opportunities and resentment of compulsory service. The former represents the purely economic element of the tax and the latter the cost of the deprivation of liberty. For instance, if the best civilian opportunity open to the individual in our example paid $6,000, his economic burden would be $3,900 (or $6,000 minus $2,100); the psychic burden would be $2,000 (or $8,000 minus $6,000).

As well as being a burden on the individual, the economic opportunity cost element of the tax represents the loss in aggregate national product which results from drafting men of higher productivity than the productivity required in military service.[1] It is possible to measure the aggregate welfare loss arising from this aspect of the draft by comparing alternative civilian incomes, by age and education, of all draftees and reluctant volunteers, to their military earnings. Using a high calculation of military pay (including veteran's and all other benefits), the President's Commission on an All-Volunteer Armed Force estimated the economic component of the tax at 1.5 billion dollars.[2] Other studies, which used a less fulsome accounting of fringe benefits (on the theory that first-term personnel do not utilize them significantly), arrived at estimates as high as 3.1 billion dollars.[3] The Commission also estimated the disutility portion of the tax at $0.5 billion. Thus even where the highest possible value is given to military compensation, the total implicit tax paid by reluctant servicemen is at least two billion dollars per year. This works out to an average of $3,600 per man, or a rate in excess of fifty percent of alternative earnings. Such a rate is very high when compared to the nine or ten percent tax paid by the average citizen, especially in view of the fact that young men tend to have relatively little wealth.

In some cases, the rate is much higher. A drafted college graduate who could earn $10,000 a year as a civilian must pay tax at a rate of seventy-nine percent or more, depending on his aversion to the military. The occasional entertainer or professional athlete who is drafted, with his civilian income in six figures, must pay tax at a rate of ninety-eight percent or more; in addition, those who enjoyed his performances must do without. It would be very interesting to observe the reaction of those Americans who decry the unpatriotic selfishness of such men if they themselves were confronted with taxation at such a heavy rate.

To see the economic burden imposed by conscription,

not to mention the moral issues involved when an unpopular war is being fought, makes it easier to understand the reaction of so many young men to this institution. The overwhelming response has been labeled "the evasion mentality"; since fewer than one-third of the men coming of age each year have to undertake military service, the great majority scramble to become part of the favored group. The Selective Service System, in large part because of the oversupply of manpower, has evolved a labyrinthine system of deferments and exemptions to accommodate the overload. Classifications span the range from "eligible" to "deferred" to "exempt." While most exemptions stem from failure to meet physical and mental qualifications, many are obtainable through parenthood or hardship. Temporary deferments can be obtained by attending college or working in an approved occupation.

Because the draft influences so many young men to act differently than they would if free choice prevailed, it correspondingly diminishes real output from optimal levels and creates additional social costs as well. Men who would prefer to be working or generally "bumming around" stay in school so that they may retain their deferment: their presence adds pressure to already crowded institutions, and deprives others of a place. Men work in jobs where they are not as productive or as strongly motivated as they could be. Some marry and have children sooner than they otherwise would. The virtual exemption of married non-fathers by executive order in September of 1963, for example, led to a rise of ten percent in the number of marriages of twenty- and twenty-one-year-olds; the average age of the inductee that year was about twenty-two.

Draft-eligible men frequently have difficulty finding employment. The larger difficulties and uncertainties posed by draft-eligibility in career and personal planning are well-known. Draft-liability, like the sword of Damocles, hangs over the head of a young man as both a constant threat and a cause of a paralysis in action. Beyond personal problems the draft consumes social resources through the controversy and opposition it arouses. Groups dedicated to draft resistance and counseling have arisen in great numbers around the country. Draft cases clog the courts. Two thousand young men are behind bars because of their moral convictions, while as many as 60,000 (including wives and families), have emigrated to Canada to avoid induction.[4] The list of these costs could be extended almost endlessly. Although there is little doubt that these costs—which can be viewed as the costs of collecting the conscription tax—are very substantial, it is difficult to assign a quantitative value to them. The president's commission, however, has estimated them at approximately three billion dollars a year. While admittedly this figure is a rough one, it nonetheless gives an idea of the order of magnitude involved.

The draft is a grievously inefficient means of staffing a technically-oriented armed force. At best a temporary expedient designed to raise the vast quantities of raw untrained infantry required for ground forces in a large-scale war, the draft is wholly inappropriate to provide trained technicians in a technologically sophisticated army. Today, even as the Vietnam war continues, only fifteen percent of all Defense Department uniformed personnel are classified as ground combat, and the proportion will drop to ten percent by 1974. The overwhelming need in the armed forces today is for trained technicians: craftsmen, mechanics, missile and radar repairmen, and electronics specialists. The day that the only requirements for a good soldier were that he be able to shoot straight and march fast are long gone; the untrained rifleman is as obsolete as his musket.

The quite natural tendency for virtually all draftees and

reluctant volunteers to leave as soon as their first tour is completed results in inflated turnover rates, which exceed thirty percent per year in the Army. Because new men must replace those who do not re-enlist, an endless recycling process springs into being. More than a half-million new men must therefore be trained from scratch. Not only does this process waste a great deal of time for many men, it requires a huge expenditure of resources each year to maintain the armed forces training establishment. A full analysis of the costs involved would require far more space than available here, but it is possible to indicate some of them. Training men who will only be in the services for two years, for example, wastes about a billion dollars a year. According to a Congressional Research Services report, it cost a minimum of $6,000 to train a foot soldier. Turnover estimates for a volunteer force indicate a drop of between 150,000 and 180,000 annual accessions. Simple multiplication yields a total extra cost of between $0.90 and $1.08 billion a year.[5]

In addition to incremental training costs, the draft, through its underpricing of quality manpower, induces over-consumption and underutilization of such labor resources. Working under a budgetary constraint, it becomes profitable for the military to use more labor—especially high-quality labor—relative to capital resources to achieve a given output. More serious, however, is the tendency of the military to focus on the low initial cost of quality manpower, invest heavily in it, and then lose it to the civilian population. An example is the most succinct way to indicate the usual patterns and costs. Suppose that by means of the draft, the Army induces a bright high school graduate or college man to enlist for three years. The military puts him through both basic and specialized training for a year or even a year and a half. At this point, the enlistee starts work in a technical occupation such as electronics. Defense Department figures show that a new man is only fifty percent as effective as a fully qualified journeyman in the first year after training, and about seventy-five percent as effective in the second. Thus the individual in our example will produce between a year and one-and-one-quarter-year's worth of competent work in electronics by the time his three years are completed. Chances are at that point that he will not re-enlist, since he will have superior civilian alternatives elsewhere, and since he probably did not desire military service in the first place. At this point, the military (in this case, read general taxpayer) has spent roughly $20,000 to pay and equip this man; another $10,000 will have been spent to train him. An investment of $30,000 will have been made for work worth perhaps $10,000. In addition, the civilian economy has been deprived of the incremental productivity of this individual. Thus the real cost to the country of drafting (or inducing to enlist), training, and finally losing this individual is about $30,000, which breaks down as follows: $30,000 cost to the military, plus $7,500 foregone civilian earnings, minus $7,500 actual pay to the individual. Clearly this is not efficient, nor is it equitable as the reluctant volunteer has borne most of the cost himself.

Because of the difficulties involved in aggregating and quantifying a vast array of many small instances of draft-induced waste, as well as in predicting the quantitative impact of restructuring the military manpower incentive system in line with true cost rather than artificial subsidies, it is not possible to derive a precise estimate of draft-induced inefficiency. But when the costs of vast under-utilization of quality manpower are combined with turnover and training costs, two billion dollars is a conservative estimate. When this is added to the implicit tax on reluctant servicemen and the costs of collecting that tax, the total annual waste caused by the draft is at least five billion dollars, and probably more than seven. These figures represent real resources going down the drain, not artificial budget allocations. And probably the greatest injustice of all is that most of these resources belong to young men, who, if only from the viewpoint of their potential to the nation's economy, can least afford to lose them.

These economic costs are slight in comparison with the intangible costs of the draft. Alienation, polarization, the erosion of idealism, and lasting injuries to the unifying web of shared values basic to the country's vitality are all deepened by the draft. It is difficult for a young man who has been raised in an environment where freedom and justice have been revered as the most worthy of values to confront an institution of such palpable injustice. The draft corrupts the concept of service by coupling it to coercion and militarism. Much has been said recently of the generation gap, a phenomenon reflecting a divergence of values between youth and the "over-thirties"; it is hard to imagine an institution which could widen this gap more effectively than the draft. Reaction to the draft frequently takes the form of resentment and bitterness towards the society which has inflicted such an affront. It causes a withdrawal of the idealistic enthusiasm and commitment to social welfare to which youth has the potential to provide a regenerating, purifying force. It is the searing damage which the draft, both as an instrument of militaristic compulsion and as a patently inequitable burden, inflicts on the ethical norms of freedom and justice which is truly its greatest cost.

Having summarized the costs of the draft, we must of course deal with the cost of ending it. The cost of ending the draft is that amount by which the budget must be increased in order to provide for a given force level on a voluntary basis, without reliance on conscription. Obviously the primary component is the raise in pay levels necessary to attract the requisite number of personnel. Since a full analysis of this problem becomes both lengthy and technical, we will limit ourselves to a relatively brief analysis of the main factors involved and a demonstration that their interaction, under any but the wildest assumptions, yields very modest estimates of the budgetary expense necessary to end the draft. We will also limit ourselves to consideration of a 2,650,000-man force (the pre-Vietnam average). Smaller forces are progressively easy to man, while difficulties increase markedly as the strength rises beyond this point.

The solution of this problem is essentially an exercise in juggling supply and demand. Every year the armed forces will require a certain number of men to maintain strength; each year the citizen population will supply a certain number of volunteers, depending on conditions of military service, including pay. The problem is to determine how many men will be required (a function of the annual turnover rate); to assess the number of true (not draft-motivated) volunteers who will be forthcoming; and to determine what changes in conditions—especially pay—will equate the predicted supply with projected demand. We will look at each of these three aspects in turn.[6]

Annual requirements for the peacetime force in 1960–65, averaging 2,650,000 men, were 520,000 men. This number included 377,000 enlistments, 106,000 inductions, and 37,000 officers. The Defense Department has projected that a peacetime force of the same size over the years 1970–75 (assuming a continued draft) would require 508,000 annual accessions, made up of 417,000 enlistments, 55,000 inductions, and 36,000 new officers. The slight drop in number is a reflection of an expected increase in enlistments and corresponding decline in the number of draftees. Turnover rates in the mixed (conscript and volunteer) force tend to be quite high; draftees and draft-motivated volunteers generally leave as soon as their first tour of duty is completed. Fewer than one out of twenty draftees re-enlists. While not at all surprising, this fact implies that turnover in an all-volunteer force, where compulsion is absent, will be significantly lower. In addition, the replacement of two-year terms by the longer regular enlistments reduces annual requirements.

It is difficult to predict the exact re-enlistment rates of an all-volunteer force, but nonetheless possible to get an approximate idea. One analyst[7] viewed the observed re-enlistment rate of first-term volunteers as a weighted average of the rate of both true and reluctant (draft-motivated) volunteers. If the observed re-enlistment rate is 22%, and that proportion which is draft-motivated is assumed to have the same re-enlistment rate as draftees, then the re-enlistment rate of true volunteers is found to be 33%. Translating this figure into turnover rates and deriving annual required accessions, we find a 29% drop, from 508,000 to 362,000. This figure is almost certainly an overstatement, since the re-enlistment rates of true volunteers in a fully professional force, with greater unit cohesiveness, career identification, and *esprit de corps,* would be higher than the rate observed in a mixed force in which morale was plagued by the taint of compulsion. Re-enlistment rates at the second term and beyond, for example—the present volunteer force—have averaged 87%.

It seems probable that retention rates in a wholly volunteer army would more nearly approximate those found in the existing career force than the low first-term enlistment rates. The British, for example, experienced almost a tripling in the average length of service per man after abandoning conscription in 1960. If we project a rise to a 40% or 50%

first-term re-enlistment rate, annual required accessions drop, respectively, to 334,000 and 297,000.

At this point we are ready to analyze the projected supply of true volunteers in the absence of a draft. Classed by motivation, there are three types of accession to the armed forces: true volunteers, reluctant, i.e., draft-motivated volunteers, and inductees. Since true volunteers alone will be forthcoming in a draft-free environment, the country can no longer count on the latter two categories of recruits. The critical question, then, is what proportion of recruits are true volunteers. In order to find the answer, the Department of Defense conducted extensive surveys of first-term personnel, asking if they would have volunteered if there had been no draft. They found in 1964 that about 60% of enlistees (and 10% of inductees) would have volunteered in the absence of a draft. In 1968 the proportion had dropped to 50%, reflecting the larger number of enlistments and the Vietnam war. Since there were almost 1.3 million men beyond the first term of service (by definition true volunteers) in both periods, the addition of 50% and 40%, respectively, of the influx of first-term true volunteers raises the total of men serving freely to just under 2.1 million in each case.[8] Thus it is apparent that the increment of true volunteers necessary to maintain strength is not overwhelming; the armed forces would not diminish almost to the vanishing point if the draft were removed. In all likelihood there would be more than two million men in uniform even if no changes in pay and conditions of service were to accompany phase-out of the draft.

In terms of annual accessions (returning to the peacetime period), the surveys indicate that roughly 232,000 of the 376,000 volunteers (average annual level) over 1960–65 joined freely. Among officers 21,500 of 37,300 would have entered without the draft. In addition about 10,000 inductees (many of whom volunteered for induction) would have joined even without the draft. Thus a total of 263,500 men were true volunteers. In comparison to anticipated required accessions in an all-volunteer force (362,000 to 297,000) the discrepancy is not tremendous, ranging from 33,500 to 98,500, depending on the re-enlistment rate assumption.[1] In addition, there is a factor, not fully accounted for in most analyses, which greatly reduces this gap. From 1964 to the early 1970s, there has been a tremendous growth in the number of young men of military age, as the postwar babies have grown to maturity. From 1964 to 1970–71 there has been a 37% increase in the number of seventeen to twenty-year-olds, the age group from which most enlistments come. Since there is little reason to assume a sharp drop-off in enlistment rates, a 37% rise in the eligible population implies a 37% rise in the number of true volunteers, from 263,000 to 361,000. It is quickly apparent that there is virtually no discrepancy between requirements and voluntary supply, when both population and turnover reduction are taken into account.

There are several qualifications to this rosy picture, which we will treat shortly, but the general conclusion, that the discrepancy between requirements and voluntary supply will be small, holds firm. The assumption of a constant enlistment rate may be overoptimistic. Historically (since the Korean War) the rate has been steadily declining. While the preponderance of this fall can be explained by the equally precipitous drop in the ratio of first-term military pay to civilian pay, a certain proportion is no doubt attributable to both an increasing proportion of young men in school and college (effectively reducing the base of potential enlistees) and a changing taste function (noneconomic attitude toward military service). Even if half of the gain in population were dissipated by these trends, however, the largest gap would still be only 50,000 men a year with existing pay levels and conditions of service. The single potentially significant alteration of these conclusions could arise from a massive shift in the supply function, brought about by a sharp rise in antimilitary attitudes among potential enlistees. But the evidence suggests that this is not the case; furthermore, to the extent it is real, chances are that a rebound would occur once the war ended and that tremendous source of unpopularity for the military were removed. As mentioned earlier, the 1968 draft motivation survey indicated that 2,084,000 servicemen were true volunteers, 30,000 more than in 1964. This is a remarkable finding in view of both the lack of progress, limited objectives, and unpopularity of the war.

Another reform which could lead to large increases in enlistments is a revamping of the recruiting system. Chronically underfunded and understaffed, this organization has limped along under the protective umbrella of the draft. With the draft ready to provide all the men it required at no more than the stroke of a pencil, the Army has had no incentive to set up a vigorous and aggressive recruiting program. Even with the tremendous manpower requirements of the Vietnam war, the percentage of the manpower budget devoted to recruiting has remained constant, while the number of recruiters, hovering at the 7,000 level, has declined as a proportion of active duty strength.

Extensive studies show that very significant gains in recruiter productivity are possible through both a reorganization of the existing system and a very moderate increase in funding.[9] The present operation, for example, functions under a rigid quota system by which a recruiter's goals are set at low levels and which, more seriously, provides absolutely no incentive for him to surpass his given goal. The creation of a graded incentive system, similar to a corporate salesman's, would undoubtedly have a tremendous vitalizing effect on recruiter productivity. Past experience shows that while the great majority of recruiting districts meet their quotas, those that fall short attain an enlistment rate 20% higher than their "successful" counterparts. The present recruiting system is clearly at a very low point on the curve of market saturation. Even the allocation of existing resources, above and beyond their insufficiency, is far from optimal. Partly for historical reasons, the majority of recruiters are stationed in small towns and rural areas. Yet by far the greatest potential enlistment area is in urban areas. Studies have shown both that the productivity of existing recruiters in those areas exceeds that of their rural counterparts, and that very large gains are possible through the addition of more recruiters. An increase of $20 or $30 million in the recruiting budget, though a pittance in the total Defense budget, would probably raise the enlistment rate at least 15% or 20%. In numbers of recruits this works out to about forty or fifty thousand, a very significant portion of any potential gap between supply and demand.

Just as recruiting languished under conscription, the pay of first-term personnel fell far behind that of careerist and civilian. From 1948, the year the peacetime draft was inaugurated, until 1965, the pay of personnel increased only 4% (an annual average of less than 0.25% a year) while the pay of longer service personnel rose by 45%. Apparently Congress felt that the authority to draft obviated the need to pay fairly. The same comparisons extended through 1969 shows rises of 60% and 111% respectively; while some of the discrepancy has been removed, the pay of first-termers is still very low, $125 a month to start. Including full value for income in kind (room and board) plus allowance for tax advantage, the average annual income over the first two years is still only $3,000, just over half what a man of comparable education and age could earn as a civilian.[10] Equity alone demands that this disparity, brought about solely by conscription, be removed. In addition the very low levels of first-term pay have become a great deterrent to men who feel an inclination to enlist, regardless of motive. To raise pay to a level more nearly in line with civilian opportunities would undoubtedly have a strong positive impact on the enlistment rate.

Several detailed econometric analyses have been undertaken to determine the precise impact of a change in military (relative to civilian) pay on the enlistment rate. The results show that the enlistment rate will increase by from 1.0% to 2.2% in response to a 1.0% change in the ratio of military to civilian pay, with the more probable values found in the middle of the range. Using the conservative value of 1.25% for the elasticity of supply, we find that an increase of 60% in pay in first-term pay yields a 75% increase in the enlistment rate, more than sufficient to cover any anticipated shortfalls. Such an increase, highly desirable on equity grounds alone, would remove the present two-year discontinuity in the military pay schedule and remove the deterrence effect of present low wages, thereby allowing men to serve without suffering undue financial penalty.

This pay raise, virtually the same as recommended by the Commission, would cost roughly two billion dollars (depending on the proportion of troops in the first term). An additional half-billion dollars would be required for medical services, the reserves, recruitment, and special pay for scarce skills, again as recommended by the Commission. There would be a considerable offset in savings, however, especially once the transition had been completed. As discussed earlier, the draft causes substantial inefficiency within the military itself. Extra training expenditures of one billion dollars are only part of the total waste we have estimated at greater than two billion dollars. As well as reflecting real resources, these draft-induced costs also appear in the budget; they would therefore diminish over time as the draft's incentive effects disappeared and act as an offset to the first-term pay raises. Even in the first two years after draft repeal substantial savings would accrue, especially as fewer men were trained. In addition, the significant number of men in noneffective or transient status would be sharply reduced; in fact an all-volunteer force of effectiveness equal to a mixed force would require 5% fewer men. Similarly a true costing approach would lead to the substitution of civilians in many positions now manned by servicemen. In both cases substantial budgetary savings would result.

There are several other sources of savings. With a 30% fall in the number of new veterans, a savings in the neighborhood of 0.3 billion dollars would result.[11] The more productive employment of men presently drafted or induced to enlist would lead to higher income tax receipts for the Treasury. Similarly 10% or 15% of all pay raises to military personnel would be returned as income tax. When all these offsets are taken into account, the budgetary expense on balance of ending the draft comes close to zero, and as efficiency savings become fully realized, would in all likelihood actually become a net savings in the future.

The draft is such a wasteful method of manning the armed forces that it would save the country billions of dollars to end it, not to mention the many intangible burdens. The question we must ask is not, "Can we afford to end the draft?," but, "Can we afford *not* to end the draft?" Obviously we cannot.

NOTES

1. This estimate is offset to the degree that first-term wages must be raised to man a volunteer force of equal effective size. *See* Stewart W. Kemp, *Crisis in Military Manpower,* ch. 5–6.

2. *The Report of the President's Commission on an All-Volunteer Armed Force* (Washington, D.C.: U.S. Government Printing Office, 1970), p. 26.

3. Ibid., p. 139.

4. Based on Canadian immigration figures.

5. Kemp, *Crisis in Military Manpower,* ch. 5–6.

6. Ibid., 6.

7. Walter Y. Oi, "The Costs and Implications of an All-Volunteer Force," in *The Draft,* ed. Sol Tax (Chicago: University of Chicago Press, 1967), p. 221 ff.

8. *The Report of the President's Commission,* p. 51.

9. Stewart W. Kemp, "U.S. Military Recruiting," Staff Paper for the President's Commission on an All-Volunteer Armed Force.

10. *The Report of the President's Commission,* p. 52.

11. Kemp, *Crisis in Military Manpower,* p. 117.

Chapter 9

Military, Civilian, or Popular Control

It is extraordinary that in an age when violence tends to dominate, those who seek ways to defuse that violence or control it are considered either harmless fools or dangerous fanatics. They are "fools" if they counter the atomic might of the superpowers with nonviolent protest. They are "fanatics" if they employ counterviolence, however pitiful or limited, in an attempt to destroy or obstruct the war machine. Even if the myth of the worldwide Communist conspiracy were true, one would think the very existence of weapons of complete destruction would merit serious concern. One would assume that a major proportion of the intellectual and organizational energies of the society would be given over to finding ways to control weapons and to resolving the great power impasse which perpetuates the continued nuclear threat. It would seem the height of folly to purposely prolong a hostile world situation in which the only resolutions appear to be holocaust or the constant danger of holocaust.[1] Yet that has been the position of the governments of all the major powers. Any creative attempts at other resolution, violent or nonviolent, by the nonaligned nations or by dissatisfied groups within the great powers themselves, have been entirely suppressed or ignored—depending upon their effectiveness and notoriety.

It is equally extraordinary that the effect of the *threat* of world destruction and the necessity for constant "preparedness" to engage in total war has provoked so little discussion in American political circles. In the Soviet Union the danger of war has been used from the start to justify the failure of the revolution to produce freedom for the common man. In the United States at least the myth "life, liberty, and the pursuit of happiness" has persisted. After all, it was James Madison, not Lenin, who warned of the impossibility of freedom in a constant state of war.

There has, to be sure, been talk among intellectuals of the "warfare state," or the "garrison society," and some excellent studies exist to show just how far America's mighty war machine has already altered the institutions as well as the social and power structures of our society. Yet these have had virtually no effect within the government. In fact they are given little serious attention even by those in America's small but vocal extraparliamentary opposition, the "movement." The critics on the left often speak of the "imperialism" and the "oppression" of capitalism without pointing out the even deeper menace. That is the very nature of all political systems which assume a constant and total threat from without, and demand therefore constant and total allegiance from within.

It is now clear that socialist states are not immune from this vice of total power resting on the claim that enemies of the state make it necessary. Socialists of most varieties,

Communists, many liberals and other establishmentarians all assume that if the state feels itself threatened, it can take away life and liberty from any and all of its citizens. The capitalists hedge on taking away property from the great corporations, but after all, these corporations share the profit from wars and rumors of wars, and scarcely need to be whipped into line. Indeed, the profit-taking of those corporations which have many defense contracts runs deeper than that of the classical capitalist corporation, for not only do the defense-oriented corporations receive large sums of money for their work, but they also receive from the government the use of public property, tools, and capital for their ventures. The property as well as the person of the individual, however, are fully expendable if a threat to the state seems to demand it.

Even Michael Harrington, whose contribution to humanism and democracy is well-known, falls into this doctrine of socialist states in his recent article approving the draft. It would be fair, he asserts, to force young men to kill and die for their country, if *all alike,* regardless of social or economic class, were made to go.[2] This is, to be sure, a doctrine of equality, but it is the equality of slavery, not liberty.

A system based on liberty assumes that the citizens themselves will decide when war is needed to defend their rights. There has never been a democratic nation which has successfully defended itself using compulsion. Although some democracies or partial democracies have resorted to the draft in time of war, the draft has never been the primary stimulus for arming the nation. Patriotism cannot be bought, but neither can it be forced. If a state must resort to force against its own citizens in order to defend itself, that state can by definition no longer be libertarian or democratic, in the sense that those words hold in the American constitutional tradition. Yet today the draft continues to be sup-

ported, after twenty years in peacetime use, not only by
arch reactionaries and racists, but also by some liberals as
"necessary for the national defense." They would equalize
its application, perhaps, but they fail to see how central it is
in the decay of that individual freedom we claim to defend
in America. How foreign and un-American to them must
seem the plea of the very American Henry David Thoreau:

> If a thousand men were not to pay their tax bills this year,
> that would not be a violent and bloody measure, as it would
> be to pay them and enable that State to commit violence and
> shed innocent blood. . . . Is there not a sort of blood shed
> when the conscience is wounded? Through this wound, a
> man's real manhood and immortality flow out, and he bleeds
> to an everlasting death.[3]

The defense of the draft and of various other measures
to control or repress citizens and their views is astoundingly
similar whether one hears it from a Soviet official or an
American leader. At a party recently, I spoke at length
with a member of the editorial staff of *Izvestia* about the
draft and about "law and order." Obviously, he said, the
American draft is unfair—it is bound to rely upon class
inequalities, but if it could be made to be truly universal, it
might be one way of regaining the respect for law so lack-
ing in Washington. He went on to decry the crime in our
capital and to urge us to institute prompt measures to bring
discipline to the youth and to keep "certain criminal elements" out of trouble. That same week, I read the speech
of Vice President Agnew before the Governors' Conference,
in which he urged us to pay no attention to those who stress
individual freedom at the expense of "collective freedom."
With the world divided into mighty armed camps, the effect
has not been surprising; all societies have been militarized to
a frightening degree, adding to the already overpowering

trends in modern technology and economy (whether state socialism or state capitalism) toward a tyranny the likes of which, the subtle but cruel forms of which, and the practically irreversible power of which, even Hitler could not have imagined.

Despite the compelling logic that war has always demanded—the domination of power by the few and the suspension of the rights of the many—and in particular the necessity of resorting to increased control of the economy and the public to gain support for an ongoing and confusing "cold war," very little attention has been given to the problem of maintaining as much freedom as possible under the circumstances. It is as though every attempt to save a bit of freedom contained an implicit attack on the war-ready state and could be used to aid and comfort our enemies. The "garrison state" is spoken of as an accomplished fact in one breath, and traditional political liberties in the next. We have come to assume that nearly three-fourths of our federal budget will be spent for military purposes; yet we forget what that means in terms of actual influence and control in the whole society. We know that the most important decisions—the top levels of politics as C. Wright Mills calls them—are made no longer by the politicians or the various public interest group leaders (political parties, unions, etc.), but by hidden groups of military men, violence experts from the federal bureaucracy, and corporation heads. Yet we continue to act as though we live in a democracy where political parties flourish and public opinion is king. We know of the "hidden persuaders," for instance, but we somehow forget them when we assume the effect of this or that politician or political issue (like the draft) on the public mind. Too often our liberal leaders are satisfied with a brief rehearsal of the inroads made into democratic form by the modern warfare state, only to affirm the necessity of its continuance. Senator Edward M. Kennedy's report on the draft is a case in point:

> Individual liberty is perhaps the fundamental hallmark of our free society. Any abridgement of this liberty stands in contravention of the traditions of democracy. . . .
>
> We must be mindful of William Pitt's statement that "necessity is the plea for every infringement of human freedom. It is the argument of tyrants; it is the creed of slaves." But the wheel of freedom is finely balanced between the interests of the individual and that of his society. In a different world than we know today, we can structure our institutions differently, and we should. But for the present, I believe we must keep the draft in our laws.[4]

Or take the warnings of the brilliant establishment political scientist, Raymond Aron. Admitting the existence in the west as well as in the east of the "garrison state," he asks:

> Will not the menace of a third world war compel even the democracies to renounce certain liberal institutions? We are observing the consequences for the democratic regimes of the quasi-war which the totalitarian states are carrying on in time of peace. These consequences are obvious: economic planning on a national scale, and the tightening up of social disciplines. . . . Let the cold war be prolonged for some years, and all countries will be transformed into fortified camps.[5]

Aron makes no attempt to soften this process. He is not the least interested in ways to minimize the "tightening of social discipline," nor does he entertain the possibilities of reshaping the conflict from its present total form, of viewing the conflict from other perspectives, or of resolving the conflict by nonviolent, diplomatic or economic means. For him, as for most scholars and politicians whether "liberal" or "con-

servative," in the last analysis, it is "red or dead." Much
lip service has been given ever since Fulbright's *Old Myths
and New Realities* to a less rigid approach to world politics.
Presidents Johnson and Nixon tell us that the world can no
longer be divided into monolithic blocs, that the Soviets are
rational men who can be dealt with accordingly, that we
must seek better and closer ties with the socialist states. In
fact, the government acts as though it no longer believes its
own rhetoric. There are evidences everywhere—from Cuba
to Czechoslovakia and from Greece to Nigeria—that the
two giant states have a tacit agreement to keep out of each
other's way. More aptly put, it is now plain to the leaderships of both countries that the Soviet Union is no threat to
anybody but her own citizens and the citizens of the states
unfortunate enough to form her buffer zone.

However, in terms of the impact of American military
posture on the American society, nothing has changed. Or,
rather, there has continued a geometric increase in the
power of the military-industry-government complex. The
United States' military budget is now larger than those of
the U.S.S.R., China, France, and West Germany combined!
The government, mostly on one military excuse or another,
spends yearly more than one-fourth of the gross national
product on defense—more than the equivalent spending for
East Germany. Between one-fourth and one-third of the
corporate profits in America are now made in connection
with military or military-related contracts.[6] And the Secretary of Defense can still appeal for massive missile and
other military build-ups on the basis of the frightening
danger of a possible Soviet superiority in some specific program. The threat of China appears at once even more
absurd and yet compelling. The image of 800,000 armed
Chinese ranting Maoist phrases is still used to instill fear in
this nation, yet the puny military expenditures and the

practically infinitesimal Chinese gross national product and growth rates are generally acknowledged. Even the former Secretary of Defense, Mr. McNamara, when questioned about a declaration of war, asked, "Against whom should we declare war?" Perhaps it is, after all, Vietnam with her 20 million people, that is the enemy—in Laos, in Cambodia, in Thailand, as well as in South Vietnam. It certainly does not speak well of the efficiency of our own huge force that we must arm to the teeth to oppose that tiny faraway land, but if it is North Vietnam that threatens us in Southeast Asia, then who is the threat in Latin America, Africa, Europe, and the rest of Asia?

The fact is the United States is the most powerful state in the whole history of the world, both in an absolute sense, and in relation to contemporary states. There is no threat to us, no challenge to our national interest. Yet, in order to "defend" ourselves, we are committed to a system of "national security," introduced in 1947, which has come to control the national priorities and much of the national economy. In the process we have lost over 100,000 American lives; we have caused the destruction of at least two million and perhaps as many as four million non-Americans. And, where we were invulnerable in 1947 to a sudden and sporadic attack, the unlimited arms and missile race has made all nations including America equally vulnerable to quick nuclear destruction. What kind of defense policy can that be for the nation whose arsenal equals that of most of the rest of the world?

The reason for such a military policy can scarely be found abroad; rather, the causes are domestic. The great military-government-industry bureaucracy came into being because of the near-total mobilization of World War II (when 40% of our GNP was committed to defense). The heroic success of the American military—including the spectacle of the atom—bedazzled and filled many of our citizens with a great pride, and led them to trust military solutions and to support continued military preparedness. While there was a demand for reduction in manpower, Americans generally supported continuation of a large military establishment—and a huge majority favored continuing peacetime conscription, or converting it to universal military training. A Roper survey in May 1946 showed 52% disapproving of the military demobilization and desirous of increased military strength. Gallup polls from 1948 to 1950 showed a two-to-one edge favoring increases for all services. Universal military training was shown to be supported by between 60% and 80% of the public between 1945 and 1956.[7] By the end of the war, the armed forces were among the largest American advertisers, and their message of patriotism and protection against evil enemies had penetrated deep into the American mind. The military had become accustomed to selling its products on the home market. By 1969 over 10,000 men were employed full-time by various military and security agencies, with countless other thousands of reserve and active duty officers employed part-time in conducting junkets and seminars or otherwise wooing the press, local and state officials, prominent American personalities and the public at large. This public relations effort was much streamlined and greatly upgraded during the reorganization of the defense establishment under Eisenhower and Kennedy along corporation lines.

There were other precedents set and lessons learned in World War II which set thus-far irreversible trends. One of the most far-reaching of these was the increased acceptance of a huge espionage network extended to the United States itself as well as abroad, and the tendency to rely on secret, manipulatory, and violent forms of power overseas to impose the will of the United States without the niceties of formal policy or official relations or the inconvenience of admitted military operations. The OSS was not dismantled but became the CIA, keeping its unique position of total secrecy—even to budget and personnel. Not only has this carryover from the war created in America reluctance to oppose military policy too vigorously; it has produced major and usually tragic foreign policy commitments. George McT. Kahin told members of the 1969 Congressional Conference on the Military Budget and National Priorities of a "whole labyrinth" of such situations including extremely serious foreign policy and military commitments in Burma, Thailand, and Indonesia.

> I could give you a whole catalogue of live and dangerous situations today in the Southeast Asia area, all attributable to decisions made without minimally necessary knowledge of relevant political factors, decisions made . . . without any knowledge of Congress and decidely counterproductive to immediate or long-term American interests.[8]

The executive himself as well as various military and security agencies undertook broad and totally new policies under cloaks of secrecy, often committing or reconsidering "military solutions" one would assume unthinkable for a democracy. Ralph Lapp in *The Weapons Culture*[9] quotes Stewart Alsop in the *Saturday Evening Post*, who exposed a plan put before President Kennedy just before his assassination to "destroy the Chinese nuclear plants in such a way that it will seem an atomic accident." America is only now becoming aware, despite warnings as early as 1961, of the major involvement in nascent wars in Thailand and Laos, mostly in the form of CIA mercenaries and agents disguised as AID officials.[10] For a time, the CIA, the State Department and the military were backing separate policies in

Laos. Arthur M. Schlesinger, Jr., revealed that, "the CIA station chief refused to follow the State Department policy or even tell the Ambassador his plans and intentions." [11]

Perhaps the emergency power inherited from World War II which has been of greatest significance is the expansion of secrecy and "classification." Many industries now require security clearance of all their employees, including those who have no dealings at all with classified materials; and the consequences of such clearance to the employees' privacy and freedom of speaking out on public policy are well known. The classified data itself becomes a haven for those who wish to hide mistakes of every kind; but worse, it hides the steady extension of power so rigorously pursued by most national security organizations. With the power inherent to manipulatory control of classified information, the defense department has a distinct advantage over would-be opponents, for it can "accidentally leak" or "reluctantly disclose" previously classified information on whim. This type of disclosure, with the added element of surprise, renders the opposition temporarily defenseless, and the momentum which is accrued by the Pentagon, before contrary arguments and evidence can be accumulated, often serves to discredit, and thereby completely squelch, the opposition. Several speakers, including Hans Morgenthau, Marcus Raskin and Herbert York, at the 1969 Congressional Conference on National Priorities, labeled secrecy one of the greatest obstacles in countering the Pentagon. Congressmen complained that they had far more difficulty getting classified data than did the defense industry executives, "and if we can't get the facts we can't make the decisions." [12] The combined force of military public relations and secrecy frightened even some of the military apologists, like the authors of *Military Sociology* who are generally most sympathetic to the military, who wrote:

So formidable are these public relations efforts that they overshadow any effort by other groups to put forth different views on the matters with which they deal. Indeed, no other group in the society is so well prepared to present its views on national security and related topics." [13]

Such problems have increasingly led to the rise of a new "power elite" in the bureaucracy of the executive government, the military and the industry, who are privy to a set of "facts" that cannot be fully known by the "public," but which cannot be challenged. As C. Wright Mills pointed out, "publics" in the optimistic liberal sense of a "free market of ideas" could not hold out long under such conditions. The interest groups on which those publics were based also became compromised and began to cease to have separate existences except in the middle and lower ranges of public policy. Labor unions had staunchly opposed conscription and military expenditure until World War II. During and after the war they became tied to "defense" jobs until today nearly four million are employed in jobs connected with national security, and another twelve million work for industries which have contracts with the defense department that amount to one-fifth or more of their total profits. Their lobbyists, with few exceptions (like the UAW's work against the ABM), are now committed to working for defense contracts, not against them, and no major unions have taken a public stand against the draft, although a few labor leaders have remained true to their earlier positions. Likewise, the leaders of the business community—once characterized as isolationist and "business pacifists"—have ceased to play their important role in balancing the power of the military and the federal bureaucracy. As early as 1944, Charles E. Wilson (the "GE Wilson"), foresaw a drastic change in government-industry relations. He proposed an alliance of military, the large corporations and the executive branch of goverenment, which has since become the most important political reality of the American scene. He wanted a "permanent war economy" in which Congress would be demoted to a peripheral role of approving funds after projects had been begun by a partnership of government and industry.[14] With the full participation of the major corporations in the profits of "national security" and with the percentage of American businesses with interests abroad that had to be protected increasing seven-fold from 1940 to 1965, no barrier to the growth of the "economy of death" remained.[15]

The universities and scholars in general participated likewise in the growth of the garrison society. It was natural that they, too, would carry over the assumptions of patriotic support in war to the new age of cold war preparedness. With practically every major scientific and social science center in the nation involved in research and development, and with most of the intellectual community committed to the "liberal" view of the world that grew out of a war executed by a New Deal administration, scarcely a voice was raised against the growth of power of the security complex. It was only in 1968, for instance, that the American University in Washington removed from its catalogue the boast that it had "served the government and the military well since the opening of biological and chemical warfare research" at the school in 1918.

So, it is quite clear that practically everybody who shares or shared political and economic power has profited somewhat from this basic change in the orientation of American political and economic power away from life and toward death. Adam Walinsky, former aide to Senator Robert F. Kennedy, said:

Professor Galbraith for one, has recently demonstrated the extent to which our prosperity and growth have been built on a corporate system which depends in turn on the defense budget for almost all of its technological innovation and for a tremendous bulk of investment in all the most advanced parts of the economy. If this is true, and I think it would be most difficult to deny it, . . . it is as Norman Mailer once said: that we have not had prosperity, we have had a fever.[16]

The nation's economy is addicted to the drug of militarism, but it is in the area of political power that the most profound change has occurred. C. Wright Mills pointed out more than a decade ago that the politician was no longer the decision-maker, and that the pluralism of balanced interest groups and regional political parties was no longer valid for any but the middle range of politics. True political power has followed economic power to the bureaucracy, military and civilian, as well as to the corporations themselves. The military has become more like a corporation, yet the corporations have been filled with military thinking and with hundreds of top military officers who now sit on their boards or head their staffs. Lobbyists for these corporations now tend to be mostly military and government people whose agencies are intimately connected with projects in which the corporations are involved, rather than outsiders exerting an influence on government.

This book is about the draft, but not the draft alone. It cannot be. The military has come to play such a powerful role in our society that any of its policies must be considered with regard to their effects on the whole nation. More to the point, any military policy should be viewed in terms of how it increases, decreases or brings control to the military power. To be sure, there are other considerations. The particular selective service system we have is truly so bad that Daniel P. Moynihan once remarked, "if it did not exist it would be impossible to invent it." A score of excellent books as well as the findings of several presidential and congressional committees have dealt in detail with the phenomenal injustice of our present method of getting men for our wars.[17] These have shown that Selective Service has promoted a class system, deferring college and graduate students—mostly from middle- and upper-middle-class families—and falling heaviest upon those who have just begun to make it—the lower-middle-class and the upper levels of the poor.

One observer, Dr. James Lieberman, a psychiatrist with the National Institutes of Health, has spoken of this process as it relates to race as "genesthesia," a clever form of racism which consistently takes and often kills the best of the black young men, while letting off the best of the whites. Despite the position of Senator Kennedy and others that a voluntary military would be unfair to black people because it would include too many of them, virtually every black leader in the country supports an immediate end to the draft. These include Eldridge Cleaver, Congresswoman Shirley Chisholm and Congressman John Conyers, Dr. Ralph Abernathy, Roy Wilkins, and Roy Innis of CORE. Manpower studies show that new trends have been set which reduce recruitment among blacks, and further indicate that a voluntary military would be less black, not more, than the draft-based army. The 1968–1969 D.O.D. fact sheets on "The Negro and the Armed Forces" show that far more blacks are drafted than volunteer (16% as against 9.9%) and that the number of black volunteers is decreasing.

The inequity and absurdity of present laws treating conscientious objection has long been exposed, particularly the spectacle of a state which espouses separation of church and state on the one hand, and sits in judgment on the religious beliefs of its citizens on the other. Finally, the system of over 4,000 draft boards has been infamous for arbitrary and uneven rulings, for insensitivity to the problems of youth (the members are mostly in their seventies), and at times for a punitive use of the draft against dissenters.

There is also the question of the inherent evil of any institution which rapes the conscience and freedom of the individual. For very many opponents, this alone is ample reason for ending the draft at once. At a time when so revolting and immoral a war is being waged without consent of Congress, the draft becomes obnoxious because of its crushing weight upon our youth. University students and their parents and members of the peace movement have frequently resisted the draft and worked against it entirely out of such a revulsion to the war, such a compassion for youth, or such a personal response to the knowledge of its effects on individuals. This has often meant that the opponents of the draft have not considered its further effect on our society or the ramifications of its abolition. They have not thought seriously about the connection between the draft and the military-industrial-government complex which they have come to fear and despise through their contact with the war. As a result, their opposition to the draft in a particular case often breaks down as attempts to abolish the draft in general begin to take shape.

The draft repeal movement in the United States today has support from conservatives, moderates, liberals, and radicals. It also has vigorous opponents from all these political groups, with many of the liberals and some radicals fearing that the end of the draft will mean the rise of a dangerous, mercenary force posing the threat of a military takeover. Surely the draft in itself, which oppresses some of our most idealistic young men, must be opposed simply because it is wrong. A nation which calls itself democratic must seek every way possible to end any institution which is based on force. If ending the draft will bring about a military full of misfits who would threaten our democracy, that is no reason to maintain the draft where such misfits exercise total control over unwilling citizens under their command. If a voluntary military is likely to be "mercenary" it is because something is wrong with our whole society. The remedy is not to maintain another evil in the draft, but to create a society in which the military could *not* be isolated and in which the soldiers would seek only to serve and defend the institutions and values which they along with the civilians would hold dear.

Nevertheless, the fear of a dangerous professional army to replace the draft is widespread among those who seek to bring social and political progress to America. Senator Edward Kennedy, for instance, opposes ending the draft on these grounds, as does the socialist, Michael Harrington. Their fear springs from a failure to place the draft in the context of its effect on the military and its power. That is a most important endeavor in a day when military priorities have made the tasks of building a freer society nearly impossible, when the insatiable demands of the war machine have turned the possibility of common affluence into the reality of lost dreams and continued oppression. We believe, as Dr. Spock has said, that our greatest hope is our children, while the overriding threat to us all is from the militarism which crushes and kills them in Vietnam, which would regiment them here at home, and which spoils their aspirations and ours as well. It is the threat of a power beyond our control which can reach down and snatch up any mother's son—a power which instills in the citizen a paralyzing helplessness. It is the threat of a hidden league of violence experts in the military, in the government and in industry who daily arrive at decisions unknown to us now but of central importance in our lives for years to come. It is the threat of an empire of violence built on the profits of waste and destruction led by the racists in Congress and the cool managers of an economy who would be managers of social control.

Those who fear military take-over and who wish to control the military should be heard. But they are wrong when they see the common soldier-volunteer as the threat. They do not seem to notice that the structure of the military has changed mightily in thirty years or that the most formidable of the hawkers of death do not wear uniforms. As Secretary McNamara once remarked of Congress, "They are thinking of another military, one we left behind us in World War II." Military coups d'état of the traditional sort with juntas and uniformed dictators just do not fit the "postindustrial" society. A primary requirement for them, in fact, is a generally underdeveloped economy where only a tiny minority shares the wealth. Although there are still underclasses in America and great poverty, a great many people share the wealth that is generated from the so-called national security build-up.

Even congressmen have been heard to remark that they fear under a volunteer army the rise of military elites with the attendant instability and tendency of generals to intervene in politics. They often point to Latin American states as the bad examples we should not follow. It is important to point out, in the first place, that practically all of the Latin American states have maintained military conscription since the beginning of this century (the beginning of a breakdown in democracy for some of them). Their military elites and coups have occurred on the backs of miserable conscripts. This has often been true elsewhere— even in the Congo, where a dictatorship arose in connection with foreign mercenaries, the common soldiers were most frequently and illegally impressed into service, sometimes without training, for use as fodder in a particular battle. Voluntary militaries in England, Canada and Australia have never led to such militarism. Of course, those societies are not underdeveloped and they do have long traditions of political democracy. That is just the point: the modern warfare state is a very unlikely target for a traditional military take-over. Generals in the United States since World War II who have acted suspiciously in this regard have been promptly silenced—Mr. Truman had the full support of his Joint Chiefs and certainly of most of the Congress for his censorship of General MacArthur. Although the general returned from Japan like an uncrowned emperor (which he had all but been in Japan) and was greeted by huge throngs throughout the land, there was never a danger of dictatorship. Certainly the draftee had little to do with the general's inability to gain power. If anything, it was the widespread influence of the giant veterans' organizations which created his popularity back home. These groups, which consistently favor military men and policy, have been swelled by draftees from two wars to become powerful lobbies. Yet they were no real threat: the men who held the power (including many former military officers) in the bureaucracy and industry were not about to spoil their chances of a far more productive, if slower and more subtle, takeover of the nation's wealth and power.

Modern dictatorships in large and developed nations have arisen as the result of a bid for power from certain of the bureacrats and corporate interests. Hitler was used by men of those groups to fire up the lower middle classes and even students in sympathy with the growth of a mighty war-making monster. That he and his ideological cohorts later used them is not surprising, but in point of fact he did not have the support of very many leading professional military men. The most significant opposition to arise during the Third Reich was led by professional military men, and Hitler's initial strength came from the dissatisfied and disillusioned draftees from World War I who had been sent out to fight for national glory only to be forced back home in defeat where they endured two decades of inflation and national shame. One of the first acts of Hitler in 1933 was to reinstitute military conscription, indeed universal military training. Following the Prussian historian, Von Treitschke, his lieutentants called such a "citizens' army" (*Kriegsdienst des Volkes*) "the school of the nation where men become patriots." [18]

The rise of a Hitler is still all too likely in America, although here the instruments of repression have been refined for longer wear and the power elite is generally too satisfied with its successes to gamble on a quick all-out victory. One might add that our military, corporation and government leaders do maintain certain scruples about the appearances of democracy—appearances which are taken by them quite sincerely as evidence of democracy. These scruples are easily dissolved when a vital interest, like profits from napalm, is at stake, but dissolving scruples at one level does not mean abandoning the national myth supporting the legitimacy claim of the government behind which the real power centers operate. The sincerity of the violence experts and their masters in believing that they defend a democratic system against totalitarian Communism is much more of a problem than an open challange to democratic institutions from Wallace or Agnew, for it is that sincerity which often diffuses opposition to illegitimate power. A group of Young Democrats from Harvard in 1968 visited General Hershey expecting to lay him low with their criticism, only to find that he was so "charming and friendly" and "really interested in youth" they forgot "even to ask about chanelling." How much more charming might have been the real power figures behind him, the men of industry profiting from his draftees who fired their weapons, or the men of government in the Pentagon and other executive agencies who set the draft calls and plotted the foreign adventures necessary to keep the wheels of violence well-oiled! Quite likely the Harvard men knew them better than they expected; many were their fathers. To be sure, it is handy at times to allow leading generals or politicians to appear intransigent and to become so identified with an issue of war or oppression that the opposition becomes preoccupied with toppling them. Dissent is dampened with apparent victory when forces behind the scene see to it that they step down. The "resignation" of Lyndon Johnson is the classic example—which came only after many party leaders and the business and union supporters of the party made it clear they intended to shift to another cover in order to avoid disaster to the war policy.

Much of the sudden opposition to the Vietnam war from former war apologists in high places of industry and academics has become quiet under Nixon, and some critics have become public spokesmen for the president's "peace plan." Mr. Nixon, on the other hand, is determined not to become so personally involved with a war policy that he can become expendable. Attacks on government policy should not be taken personally, urged one presidential advisor to Mr. Nixon, for such a reaction invites personal defeat. At least some of the holders and managers of power would not welcome another case of popular pressure forcing a president out of office. Although it had virtually no effect on basic policy, the antiwar campaign came dangerously close to a people's movement for a change in national priorities—ABM almost fell. Ditching Johnson was an appropriate maneuver for the power elite, but a similar move only a few years later might not leave policy so unscathed. Daniel Moynihan, it is said, wrote several memos to President Nixon which have been generally heeded. In one of them he is reported to have said,

> In a sense he [Johnson] was the first American President to be toppled by a mob. No matter that it was a mob of college professors, millionaires, flower children and Radcliffe girls. . . . The nation's origins are revolutionary and there remains a tradition that gives an advantage to those who challenge authority rather than those who uphold it. . . . President Johnson took all this personally, but I have the impression you will make no such mistake! [19]

One of the guardian-planners of the Great Society is here praising the talents of the new president as one who will know his place, who will not try to rule as a personal president, but as a salesman for and convener of the national security committee—including, but much larger than, the National Security Council—which makes the big decisions and sets the priorities. At the same time the president is being warned that he could also go the way of other politicians who take their role too "personally." The case of General Hershey shows clearly the use of an unpopular figure at a lower level to cover the real evil of a system.

By allowing the movement to fuel the fire of opposition to the Director of Selective Service, the power structure achieved two ends: (1) After a sufficient build-up of public indignation against Mr. Hershey, some steam was taken out of the movement. The *New York Times,* as usual, was quick to point out how well the government had reacted to student pressures, and to note that observers believed the anti-draft momentum to be seriously affected when he was kicked "up" to a harmless position. The president feigned a struggle with the "real" hawks, Mrs. Smith and Mr. Stennis, in his attempt to bring a new image to Selective Service. His second appointment, Mr. Tar of the Air Force, is the epitome of the syrup-sweet side of American bureaucracy, which must always be a Janus with a face that snarls and a face that smiles. (2) The presence of Mr. Hershey and even some of the glaring inadequacies and injustices of the System provoked louder and louder protest, but that protest was against problems in the details and management of the system, rather than directed against the basic tyranny of the draft. This is not to say that deferments, injustice to conscientious objectors, and unfair boards did not serve very important purposes for the war elite, but their existence also served to hide the deeper evils and purposes of the system. Dr. George Wald of Harvard has called this the "equity play." Many are tricked into working for an "equitable draft," when they might have worked instead to abolish the basic injustice of the draft itself. Thus, the president with his lottery farce of old men and well-selected youth pulling death numbers from a fishbowl could play the reformer. The same procedure can be seen in the long game of the president's "secret plan," his bland television addresses amid fanfare and flourish, and his "state of the world" report which Mr. Nixon himself called the most remarkable document of twentieth-century American foreign policy (evidently remarkable because it said nothing with such great art). The hoax of "Vietnamization" is another example.

Of course, if little Hitlers can be used by the system, one day a big one may come along. In that event, the increasing centralization and control of all life-processes by the state, the ease with which the media is manipulated and its use to manipulate the masses, the network of efficient but hidden power centers outside the official channels for decision *making,* and the huge manpower of the bureaucracy directly dependent upon government, may all conspire to create the most complete and most difficult-to-topple tyranny ever conceived. If that happens in America as it happened under less sophisticated (and less dangerous) conditions in Germany, what great power will come to rescue us from our political strangulation? There will be no America to save *us*. Then conscription can be extended to every person. Universal military training is only a token of what the state will expect then. The existence of the military-industrial-bureaucratic elite and its constant accumulation of power and wealth threaten our democracy now; indeed they have already subverted it. The draft has been one tool among many to achieve these ends of control. It is a peculiar logic which somehow sees the end of the draft as a threat to a democracy already near death.

It is especially appalling that some of our liberal leaders have so misread the dangers to our freedoms. At a time when every friend of democracy should oppose our chief enemy, this power conglomerate of managers—the violence colony as Marcus Raskin calls it—which extends our malignancy across the world, promulgates the greatest violence in history, and keeps us from the great social progress which our history and our technical advance now merit, men like Senator Kennedy confine themselves to reforming the draft and warning of the dire consequences of a volunteer army. They speak of civilian control and democratization of the military, appropriate perhaps in Peru or in America in 1920, not now when the need is *popular* control of the military, the civilian bureaucracy and the corporations. Democratization can scarcely come through force, the control of citizens and the arbitrary (by lot) selection of some against their will to serve the ends of a professional military machine with its government-industrial allies. The draft in fact has a mixed impact on dissent within the army and political protest outside it (see below, chapter 10). The thorough coupling of civilian violence experts from AEC, CIA and DOD to military policy and often to explicitly military programs, and the appearance of so many former military officers in leading positions in General Dynamics, Honeywell and other security industries where a hundred billion a year is converted from tax dollars to the profits of destruction—these facts make civilian control a moot issue. They demand a quick and powerful movement for popular control of our society and its priorities.

Volunteers in the military do nothing to counter that movement—the antidraft movement provides the basis for it. Americans from right to left, from farmer to student and worker to businessman have come to despise the war and through it the draft. If the end of the draft comes at all, it will be their protest which has forced the change. The resistance, emigration and court cases connected with the draft have precedent only in the open defiance of the now defunct segregation statutes. Certainly the end of those laws did not mean the end of racial prejudice and institutional discrimination. One could argue that their existence made the issues clearer and strengthened opposition to them. Very few would argue that the laws should not have fallen simply to enable us to see better the problems of our society. Yet many do hold that the draft keeps the public aware of the evil and the aggressive military machinations of our state, and so should be kept. Not only can it be shown that this is not true, but such logic is perverse (see chapter 7). The aide of a well-known liberal senator recently put the argument this way to a delegation including the leaders, young and old, of national organizations ranging from the YMCA to the Methodist Church and the Ripon Society:

> The point is, to pay the draftees a proper salary would not only make them mercenaries, it would raise the defense budget. Now, it would be nice to think the money would come from missiles, but it will come instead from the social programs I'm sure all of us are working for. And besides,

who would protest the war if not the parents of the draftees?

Every one of these arguments betrays the deep-seated defeatism that is so much a part of American liberalism today. How strange to assume that we will have to go on paying high salaries and retirement benefits to officers of the higher ranks—and allow them to build fortunes later in armaments on the basis of their military contacts—yet must not pay the men who go off to be shot in Vietnam because that would make them mercenaries. Far more frightening, however, is the assumption that revealing the cost of soldiers (which the society really pays for already in hidden social and other costs) will produce not still more pressure to reduce the defense budget, but less likelihood of cutting down on missile spending! It is evident that many liberals have little confidence at all that the present enormous expenditure for armaments can be significantly altered. There are senators and others who preach reduction in military spending, but who are rather certain from the start that only nominal dents can be made in the military empire. These are usually in manpower, elderly ships, and useless bases that were boondoggles in the first place. Such cuts do not provide the slightest threat to the violence complex. When the Secretary of Defense leaks small reductions totaling two billion dollars over a four-month period, each time noting the total of two billion, he has done nothing more than cut out some of the waste and corruption that characterizes the uniformed military. He has done nothing to cut back military power or to allow the reallocation of funds for new priorities outside the national security circle. Nevertheless, his efforts have brought him rewards. Much of the attempt to reduce military spending will have been thereby coopted. Such behavior is to be expected from those who have vested interests of one sort or another in the violence complex, but frequently liberals actively cooperate in this process. They talk of corruption, inefficiency and wasted cost to taxpayers rather than the real issues. They pretend that minor cuts, or the major cuts that *almost* occurred, are of vast importance in revamping national priorities. By these expectations and actions, they fulfill their own prophecy. The terror and the violent power that confronts us all are not themselves confronted.

Are the liberals not suspect of some vested interest of their own? After all, liberals invented the myths of anti-communism to keep the military build-up going after World War II. After a slowdown under Eisenhower, liberals from academic circles (like the Michigan State professors who aided Diem) and from the outgoing New Deal bureaucracy revived enough "crises" to make it necessary to "close the missile gap" and start again the rise of "security" costs. It was John Kennedy whose rational approach brought consistency for the first time at least since Teddy Roosevelt to our foreign policy. It was he who saw the logical necessity of following through on nuclear threats. It was he who sponsored the sharpest rise of all in military appropriations and involvements abroad. To be sure, the CIA had already embroiled us in at least a score of "danger spots" around the world (dangerous usually because we were there), and it is also true that they often misled Kennedy both about objective facts in the field and about their own intentions. Yet the liberal Democratic administrations of Kennedy and Johnson saw the real escalation set in, both in Vietnam and in the power of the violence complex at home.

To return to the pessimism of the particular liberal aide above, it is depressing to realize how little change he expects. Since his pessimism has not led him to severe frustration or revolution, we must only assume he has not

judged the seriousness of the malaise correctly. His faith in
the American people is equally low, for he is sure that the
only protest to expect is that of the immediate involvement of draftees and their parents. In another more political context he might be expected to exaggerate the growth
of dissent as evidence of the popularity of his own views.
The force of involvement alone rarely leads to protest, but
rather to acquiescence—as the Germans say, "you get used
to everything." Only if there is already a deep disturbance,
a mistrust of the leadership or a feeling that things have
somehow gone wrong does involvement lead to dissent
rather than to pride and patriotism. If the nation is at last
disturbed, awakened to the sickness of artificial prosperity
based on violence, it is largely because of Vietnam. No one
would suggest continuing Vietnam for that reason—not least
because even the horrors of Vietnam after a while may *have*
to be accepted by most people (as My Lai so quickly was),
simply to avoid what is the most difficult thing a man can
ever do: to question everything without hope of an answer.
If we are to be able to throw off the yoke of a growing and
self-sufficient violence complex, Vietnam will have helped.
The draft will have played a role: but a much greater role
in reasserting popular control of military and civilian bureaucracy alike, and of giving back to the people the feeling
of their own power to produce meaningful change, will have
to be assigned to the present popular movement to end the
draft and to refashion all our institutions for new purposes.

One reason for the importance of the draft-repeal debate
is that it points up the paucity of so much of the opposition
to the war, and to the national security state. The radical
speaks of imperialism, but does he always remember the
nature of the new imperialism and how it differs from the
old? Despite his best intentions, the various doctrines which
have used imperialism continue to play a role in the mean-

ing of that word, and often the radical still has in mind the scowling general, the hopeless conservative politician or even the meddling missionary when he thinks of imperialism. The new imperialism is not as much motivated by the traditional exploitation of the poor, as it is by a bureaucratic intervention into the affairs of the "less fortunate members of the free world"; an intervention which has as its raison d'être the extension of that same bureaucracy, and the justification of its continued existence and increase of power at home. Just as a war from time to time justifies the power of the military, and just as continual preparation for war is even better (since war is dangerous even to military men), the bureaucracy feeds upon itself. As it grows abroad ever further into the lives of other nations and as it grows at home ever deeper into the lives of citizens, it rationalizes its own growth.

To those who have read the works of Strachey, Raskin, Waskow, Barnett, Irving Howe or other shrewd observers of the modern imperialist scene, these facts are well known. But for many of those who use words like "imperialism" in the arena of politics the change has penetrated only superficially. It is difficult to remember that liberals frequently share in the new imperialism, while conservatives (among them even some "old Republicans" and generals) may be among the newly dispossessed. Most of the old-fashioned businessmen who have been replaced by the new state corporations do not know it yet, but there are some in the business world, as Richard Barnett rightly points out in *The Economy of Death,* who have noticed the difference. Here and there are traditionalist politicians following suit. At least several military officers have taken up the call to control what General Dale Orville Smith called the "defense intellectuals." [20] As we saw above, the liberal on the other hand is often so compromised by the warfare state system, that he is afraid to try too hard to hasten its demise, or he is just not willing to admit the depth of the problem. He speaks instead of minor organizational changes here and there, or of throwing the rascals out. It was almost in this vein that Senator Gaylord Nelson spoke at the congressional conference in early 1969:

> . . . the problems will come under control as soon as we throw everybody out of office who is not interested in bringing them under control. And that will happen pretty soon, and the sooner the better." [21]

Speaking at that same conference, Charles Schultze candidly admitted his own feeling that no thoroughgoing reform of the society was needed. He suggested instead that the American people deserved some new institution that would provide them with the now unavailable information on which they could make "fundamental choices with respect to their weapons systems and military decisions." At that same conference, Marcus Raskin who spoke of the "national security state" pointed out the rub in this approach:

> I remember that some of the people sitting at this table suggested the idea of a disarmament agency. I drafted a bill and came to serve in the White House as the point of contact on that issue. And the disarmament agency, which was to sit as the vested interest for disarmament in the Government, turned out to be nothing at all. The problem, if you go the organizational route, is to find something which will not turn out to be nothing. [22]

Just how "nothing" the disarmament agency is, is illustrated by the clause creating it which forbids it to propagandize, although millions of private and public dollars and thousands of private and public employees are provided yearly to blow the horns of armament.

The threat of the civilian-operated, military-run and industry-backed violence complex is so very great today and its impact so immediate and so final for those who are destroyed by it in Vietnam, repressed by it in Chicago or neglected by it in Alabama, that the folly of these approaches has become acute.

NOTES

1. If the danger is not real or believable as an impending possibility, the entire "deterrence system" fails to work. Nuclear war must remain a live option, if it is to work to keep nuclear war from occurring. President Eisenhower thus blundered when he assured the Russians *we* would not use our weapons first under any circumstances; and the Kennedy, Johnson, and Nixon administrations have appropriately made clear the revised American doctrines of first strike and preemptive war. *See* Herman Kahn, *On Thermonuclear War* (Princeton, N.J.: Princeton University Press, 1961).

2. *Washington Evening Star,* March 3, 1970.

3. Henry David Thoreau, *On the Duty of Civil Disobedience* (New York: Rinehart & Company, 1960).

4. "Statement of Senator Edward M. Kennedy," *A Study of the Selective Service System: Report of the Senate Subcommittee on Administrative Practice and Procedure* (Washington, D.C.: U.S. Government Printing Office, February 1970), pp. 87, 91.

5. Raymond Aron, *The Century of Total War* (Boston: Beacon Press, 1954), pp. 89–91.

6. *See* "Military Balance, 1966–67," Institute for Strategic Studies, London, page 8. *See also* yearly reports from the Institute.

7. Samuel P. Huntington, *The Common Defense* (New York: Columbia University Press, 1961), pp. 236, 240.

8. George McT. Kahin, "Small Secret Decisions Often Generate Crises," *The Progressive* (vol. 33, no. 6, June 1969), p. 32.

9. Ralph Lapp, *The Weapons Culture* (New York: W. W. Norton, 1968), p. 75.

10. *Washington Post,* March 10, 1970, p. 1.

11. Arthur M. Schlesinger, *A Thousand Days* (Boston: Houghton-Mifflin, 1965), p. 326.
12. Lester L. Wolff, "Do We Have a National Purpose?" *The Progressive*, June 1969, p. 29.
13. Charles H. Coates and Roland J. Pellegrin, *Military Sociology* (University Park, Maryland: Social Science Press, 1965), p. 56.
14. Fred J. Cook, *The Warfare State* (New York: The Macmillan Company, 1962), p. 76.
15. The most recent and profound treatment of the rise of the warfare state or national security state is *The Economy of Death* by Richard J. Barnett (New York: Atheneum, 1969). Other earlier studies include: John Swomley, *The Military Establishment* (Boston: Beacon Press, 1964); Fred Cook, *The Warfare State* (New York: The Macmillan Company, 1962); and Ralph Lapp, *The Weapons Culture* (W. W. Norton & Co., Inc., 1968). The latter includes a handy guide to corporations, agencies, universities, and individuals involved in the military-industrial complex.
16. Adam Walinsky, "Do We Have a National Purpose?" *The Progressive*, June 1969, p. 24.
17. *See* Sol Tax, *The Draft* (Chicago: University of Chicago Press, 1967); American Friends Service Committee, *The Draft?* (New York City: Hill and Wang, 1968); and *The Report of the President's Commission on an All-Volunteer Armed Force* (Washington, D.C.: U.S. Government Printing Office, 1970).
18. Friedrich Ruge, *Politik, Militär, Bündris* (Stuttgart: Bündris Rowahlt, 1963), p. 6.
19. *Washington Evening Star,* March 11, 1970, p. 6.
20. Dale Orville Smith, *The Eagle's Talon* (Washington: Spartan Books, 1966).
21. Senator Gaylord Nelson, "Why Youth Raises Hell," *The Progressive* (vol. 33, no. 6, June 1969), p. 52.
22. Marcus Raskin, "Political Realities," *The Progressive* (vol. 33, no. 6, June 1969), p. 55.

Chapter 10

After the Draft Is Ended

In each of the preceding chapters we have asserted that the draft can and should be repealed. We have pointed out the centrality of the draft to the problems of a growing militarism in America and its importance in restoring the emphasis in our society on individual freedom. We have indicated that a war atmosphere has poisoned our social and political environment as much as the pollution caused by a growth-conscious industry has poisoned our physical environment. We have maintained that a voluntary military is the only kind compatible with a return to freedom, and that it will not present new problems for the society as a threat to democracy. We have shown that any military is a threat to a free society, and that our present military-government-industry alliance is especially dangerous. The task that remains is to suggest why the present set-up is so problematic, how it differs specifically from the classical position of the military within the society, and how it may be contained, controlled, and eventually reduced in its hold on our nation.

Before we examine these questions it is good to remember what has been repeated often in various forms in the earlier chapters: the nation-state system itself demands that the state be accorded absolute loyalty. Absolute loyalty of all men within artifical geographical boundaries can never be achieved and can only be approximated by ruthless force and by allowing all power to gravitate to the center of the state. That process is inimical to freedom. The nation-state is also bound to make war. As soon as it establishes absolute loyalty to itself within its boundaries (or an approximation or appearance of it), it is bound to set out upon a course of "defense" involving technological progress and weapons stockpiling. That course must lead to an ever-expanding notion of the limits of national interest, and in a crowded world those limits will soon infringe upon the expanding limits of some other state. The battles of "national interest" that ensue are competitions in technology which may have been useful for "pure scientific progress," but which ceased to have any utility for humanity when "progress" advanced to the sublime point where the destruction of all men became possible.

Of equal importance to the progress of the technology of destruction which has accompanied the growth of the nation-state has been the progress of the technology of domination. That, too, has now reached the level where mankind cannot possibly be served by greater efficiency in human domination and social control. Such a statement, of course, involves a value judgment: that man will cease to be human when he is totally controlled, however meek or lovely may be the automated product. Since the very nature of the nation-state is its call for total "service" and its ability to make war in its own interest, obviously no free society can long survive the rigors of nation-statehood. Hegel pointed out that "wars between states do not flow from outside events, but from the finitude and incompleteness of states," and that wars were demanded by a system of "sovereign" but limited states.[1] Hegel then justified his own defense of the nation-state with its centralizing bureaucracy by praising the function of war as "a storm which purifies the stagnant waters," giving strength and unity to the people of each nation.

It was from these Hegelian propositions that Marx derived his own certitude of the necessity of internationalism. The working class, who should rightfully proceed to inherit the modern world which their labor had built, could only do so internationally. A nation of workers maintaining the assumptions of sovereignty and national interest would be liable to the same errors of vision and frequency of wars as the bourgeosie. Workingmen could have no country. Marx was wrong: workingmen who take over a state, even for the revolutionary purpose of bringing communism to the whole world, very soon have a loyalty to what they possess, that is, to the bureaucracy they have inherited. Likewise, workingmen in a capitalist nation-state that manages to pay its workers well as a result of enslaving foreign workers will be likely to develop a peculiarly avid patriotism. Had the whole world consisted of developed capitalist nations, each exploiting its own workers, Marx's prophecy of an international workers' revolution would have been fulfilled. Uneven development produced another scenario. Workers seized control in those countries where the least efficient capitalism had developed, while an alliance between capitalists, bureaucrats and some of the worker-leadership produced various versions of the welfare-warfare state in the more advanced countries. In the rest of the world—where colonialism had kept national capitalism from developing at all—poverty increased while literacy rose, as Marx had predicted for the whole world, and revolutions became more and more likely. These would be faced not with reordering an existing industrial society, but with building it in the first place. To complicate matters still more, several former colonies were able to gain technical assistance and know-how (although often grudgingly) from the West, and thus avoid the danger of revolution, middle-class or otherwise. In such a world the working-class states developed protective national bureaucracies of their own. They became a part of the warring nation-state system.

Although socialism has the utopia of communism as its ultimate goal, both capitalism and socialism assume a common principle: productivity. In the one, it is productivity for the benefit of the few; in the other, the benefit should accrue to the many. The individual, however, as opposed either to the few or the many, a minority, a majority or even an overwhelming (and stultifying) consensus is given short shrift by both systems. In both, it is assumed that the individual's rights will be respected where possible, but that in any emergency, the good of the state (or the whole, or the collective) will be considered primary. Since the state defines the emergency the individual has no assurances or rights that are not contingent on the needs of state power. To be sure, democratic institutions in either a socialist or capitalist society provide a check on the demands of the state and see to it that the burden falls as equally as possible. It might be added that the coupling of socialism and democracy improve the situation still further by assuring that no one is rewarded unduly for his productivity. Nevertheless, democracy under nation-state conditions remains a way of structuring the will of the collective, and individuals are bound to suffer. There are times when the state must make demands on some of its citizens which it cannot make on others—this is the situation of selective service both in the United States and in the Soviet Union, where some are chosen to fight or die and others to study or work in essential industries. If there are not enough willing to contribute to the productivity necessary for destruction, then some must be conscripted.

In the United States, the selection has been by a complicated and often unfair process of local boards, with equally complicated legal provisions for some of those with conscientious objections. The result has been spotty justice at best, the rape of youthful conscience at worst. With an increased number of those objecting and with a multiplication of motivations for those objections, the selection process is overburdened with noncooperation, and the only alternative compatible with the security of a war-prepared nation-state is one which abridges freedom: compulsion. It is interesting that the Soviet Union has found a less dependable, but in some cases perhaps more workable solution (from the point of view of the state). No conscientious objection is allowed at all, since it is assumed that any conscientious person must seek to serve the collective. This assumption obviates any consideration of individual freedom whatsoever. Nevertheless, it is known that many conscientious objectors are exempted from service each year in the USSR. I have talked to many of these young men in Moscow and Leningrad, and to even more in the non-Russian sections of the Union where objection is often based secretly on national pride or principle rather than pacifism. It seems that the Soviet state sees no benefit in forcing unwilling young men into its military establishment. If the manpower pool were to shrink below its present high level, or if the security needs of the state were greatly to increase, the Soviets would simply revert to the less efficient measure of compulsion and imprisonment—as they did in World War II. In the United States, we prefer to think we have a legal promise that that cannot occur. Yet we imprisoned several thousand Quakers and others in the last war, we are jailing and forcing into exile countless thousands now, and if we ever encounter a situation in which a sizeable minority of the population refuses to go to war for the state, there can be no doubt that rigid compulsion will be used as a quick solution. It is tempting to suspect, for instance, that the present defoliation by the U.S. of its entire border with Canada may have a use in travel control as well as in agriculture. How strange that we accept a set of laws for the conscientious objection of a tiny minority as though that were a most democratic practice, when the very nature of these laws and security demands of the state would make similar objection impossible for large minorities or for the majority.

So we see that conscription (and confiscation) are of the very essence of the nation-state democracy. In the present world arena, two great states are armed beyond the teeth to protect their sovereign interests. In pursuit of those interests, absolute loyalty is required, and the threat of abridging every freedom is always present. How then can conscription be abolished? How can freedom be feasible if it cannot be compatible with such a security? The answer is to be found in the changing consciousness of the peoples especially of the two superstates and their allies, but also of the other struggling states around the world. A change in the consciousness of the people is occurring that is related to the changed technological, economic, and political conditions. No longer are there equal nation-states seeking to protect protectable borders. The consciousness of people within those former states was of themselves as separate, and progressing under national leadership. As such they were interested in "security" as well as freedom. Control was not complete within each state, yet voluntary or pseudo-voluntary loyalty to the state paid off in terms of security from foreign (and unknown) invaders and of constantly improving services for the general welfare, while the primitive nature of the technology of domination kept the individual sufficiently undisturbed to give him the illusion of freedom too. The common defense and the general welfare were both important to the people and well within the ability of the state to provide.

The situation has now changed considerably. There are now only a few states that can be considered at all sovereign, since most others are dependent upon the great powers. In fact the second-rate powers may now have less actual sovereignty than some of the smaller states. By careful balancing acts between two or more larger powers, or by other stratagems of subterfuge, a number of small nations have maintained a large degree of control over their own development, however precarious that control may be. The second-rate powers like Britain, on the other hand, have an amazingly small degree of independence. As has been pointed out, America's nuclear umbrella over western Europe and its forced acceptance by virtually that whole region amounts to "defense" without representation. An American president, for whose election the Europeans have no responsibility whatsoever, will make the final decision to save or destroy the cities and inhabitants of Europe. Hence, the citizens of all but the great power states must find their governments wholly incapable of providing security. Since, for most of the developed ones, the common good is already an accepted standard, citizens of the advanced smaller nations are beginning to challenge the relevance of security at all. Since the "underdeveloped" nations continue to be exploited by the great powers, since their capital is constantly depleted by foreign firms, since no effective measures can be taken to stem poverty, and yet their populations are tutored in the western desires for consumer goods through exposure to western products and advertising, the citizens of these states find them incapable of providing either for security or the common good.

The most significant and unparalleled shift in the consciousness of people is occurring in the great powers themselves. It is difficult to assess the change within the Soviet Union, although recent underground writings as well as officially published literature ranging from Solzhenitsyn to Yevtushenko and Taras indicate that the popular opinion of the role of the state is undergoing significant revision. My own frequent visits to all parts of the Soviet Union and Eastern Europe have led me to believe that this revision is quite extensive, especially among students and young workers. There are the well-known incidents involving the children of prominent Polish officials during that country's brief "thaw," and the recent and surprising involvement of the children of East German party leaders in pro-Czechoslovak demonstrations. During a recent tour of Russia, I met with groups of students who openly defied their government on Czechoslovakia and Israel, and who said they had signed petitions for freedom of speech or to support dissident writers. One of them, whom I have known for some time, is the daughter of a member of the Georgian supreme court. Although she shares the prestige and economic prerogatives of her father's important position, she is a member of a large group of students at the University in Moscow who meet informally to discuss ways they can affect the administration of state bureaucracy in the Soviet Union. Their purpose is to subvert slowly a system which is practically immune to revolution because of its virtual monopoly both on the symbols of revolution and on all instruments of communications and coercion. Such a system makes violent and open revolution most unlikely, although it may invite coups d'état, depending on its internal efficiency.

The same can be said for the increasingly centralized and well-organized bureaucracy in the United States, which has step by step legitimized the use of police and even federal troops to "restore order" wherever the state feels too threatened to protest. Violent revolution is seen as an increasingly unrealistic path to radical change in the modern state by most observers of every political persuasion.[2] Attempts at such violent revolution lead generally to ruthless repression, which increases and enhances the legitimacy of the police state powers. Tightly-knit coups d'état, whether of the left or the right, may also result from secretly planned and brilliantly executed violent attacks on the nerve and power centers of the centralized warfare state, but these would necessitate secrecy and violence of such a degree that their successes would likely lead to new forms of repression rather than a reorientation of values. The very fact that they would have taken over the warfare state machinery, rather than entirely smashing it (an impossibility without world annihilation), or transforming it, would make unlikely any shift in the direction of individual freedom (see chapter 1).

On the other hand, revolution of quite another sort is an increasing possibility in the great modern empires. This revolution begins as the "youth phenomenon" discussed in chapter 1. The children of all classes, including the children of the elite, grow up with relatively and increasingly similar influences. They are all exposed to television and to approximately the same bad school situations. They are all frustrated in a number of ways by the incongruence of their goals with the society's. The goal of the state remains security, and the approved goal for the "good citizen" remains the common welfare (general economic security at minimum levels, graduated upwards according to social status and sometimes according to race). In the past, some groups at the bottom were excluded from the "common good," and served as threat and prestige incentives to the classes above them. With the shrinking of both geographical and social distance under modern conditions and communications, this method has lost its efficiency for the state, both because the excluded groups have grown articulate in their attempts to get in, and because the youth of other groups have come to demand their inclusion. Despite continued resistance from those most threatened by or most able to exploit the outcast groups, the managers of the society have decided it will be more advantageous to bring them in, primarily at the lowest levels possible. In a memo (see chapters 1 and 9) to President Nixon, Daniel P. Moynihan urged that the "Negro lower class be dissolved," so that these Negroes might become a "stable working class of truck drivers, mail carriers and assembly line workers." [3] These formerly excluded groups, however, are to be included in the goals which the state has set: national security for the state and economic security for the individual. A part of the problem which the society now finds in pursuing its "integration" policies is that black people are increasingly unwilling or uninterested in joining a white society. They are instead often more interested in freedom—in the early stages of black consciousness, group freedom, but increasingly and as they are involved with the youth from the rest of society, they seek individual freedom, the forgotten goal of our republic.

The children of the various elite groups (including a part of the working class in the United States) first discover the sham of equality under the term "common good." They uncover the most hideous roots of the race problem in social and economic inequality, but also in the violent repression of the individual rights of black people. From there it is a short step to the discovery of their own dissatisfaction with the goal of economic security based on productivity. In the "advanced" societies, economic security ceases to be an overriding concern of the youth precisely because they have come to assume it as their right, not as members of an elite group, but as human beings. They seek to extend that right to others, but their awareness of modern politics and technology is sufficiently sophisticated to include the existence of the wealth in our world which is somehow being kept from, or is so poorly distributed to, the bulk of the world's population that they continue to starve amid the affluence of large middle-class nations. Finally, this is a most politically literate generation. It proceeds from moral questions directly to politics, and vice-versa. So, they ask, what is keeping the world from the opulent fruits of man's progress which now exist?

The young find their answer in the hollow ring of the other and primary goal of their societies: national security. Under that cover they see the more powerful states continuing centuries of exploitation. They see the great powers, acting in what they call "national interest," crushing the spirit of the freedom revolutions and also often the revolutions of economic equality around the world, whether it be the USSR in Poland and Czechoslovakia, China in Tibet, or the United States in the Dominican Republic, Guatemala, and throughout Southeast Asia. They also are shocked by the sudden discovery that huge portions of the national product are used in the security games and the destruction and dominations that go with them. Even at home, they find, the price of "security" is a deteriorating "general welfare," with education, health, transportation, the cities, and conservation sacrificed for the priorities of "security."

At the same time, they learn that the constant threat to nuclear security means the exposure of all the people at all times to the threat of annihilation.

In all this process, two things have happened. The facts outlined above and the media through which they are conveyed in the modern world have produced a new "public" to replace the now defunct "publics" of business, labor, agriculture, etc., on which the theory of "democracy" rested. Those publics vanished, as C. Wright Mills pointed out in *The Power Elite,* with the increasing demands of security and the decreasing differences between the groups in their attempts to get economic security. The consensus politics of the great wars destroyed whatever pluralism of publics had previously existed. For a time—the silent fifties, the days of "the end of ideology"—publics vanished and with them all possibility of even a loyal opposition within the nation. But in the late fifties and the sixties, this new public arose based on a common dissatisfaction with the twin goals of national and economic (productivity-oriented) security, and committed to a new goal, the revival of individual freedom. A new self-conscious group has come into being to replace the various classes and publics of the past. We might call this "the people," although today it is still primarily "the youth." That is the first change.

The second change is that these people have a new consciousness based on a desire for freedom rather than security, or rather they believe their only security will lie in freedom. Based on these convictions and this vested interest in freedom (it is often a very real psychic interest, for without their freedom, they are maimed and miserable) they have begun the only popular revolution that could work under the conditions of the garrison state. They are saying "no" to participation in the security and productivity systems. Faced with the powerful oppression of the state, many of them have fled to subsystems (such as dogmatic political parties) which are just as oppressive. Others have taken the escape route of drugs. Even these methods, however, provide a real danger to the goals of the state. It is no sure thing, by any means, that angry adults will not bring about the perfection of the warfare state in order to contain their terrible children. It is not at all certain that the state will be unable, through its own manipulation of the media and the schools, to reverse the trend, and to reimmerse the young in doublethink. These are possibilities, but in the meantime, the one ground for hope, and the only reason for believing freedom to be feasible, is in the creation of a new consciousness among the people, based on the changes described above, and beginning with youth.

Our basic premise, then, is that so long as there are armed nation-states, freedom will never be safe from the inroads of security. It should, therefore, be our primary aim to move away from the goal of security and toward the goal of freedom. We have discussed why that cannot be done by a direct attack on the existing nation-states (which thrive and grow under such attacks, internal or external). There is also reason to believe it cannot be done simply by asserting the principle of international rule and constructing a new world on that basis. The great powers would coopt any such system that was built up, as they have the United Nations. Although such world structures should be encouraged, they are at the very least premature. It is our opinion that the place to begin is within the nation-state, and particularly within the great powers, to subvert the goals of these states from security to freedom by converting the pressure of the new people's (our youth) consciousness outlined above into the power to change policy. The forces of freedom (as opposed to those who stress either economic security or group security) should develop a well-planned strategy to fit every institution in the American society which now serves either the principle of productivity for its own sake or the principle of destruction for "security's sake."

To begin with the latter may be wiser. The key institutions of which we speak include the great corporations (and their destruction of our environment as well as their profits from destruction abroad and in the streets), the mass media (as they package and sell the warfare state), the local organs of "law and order" and of "education," the various government agencies (whether ICC or HUD), the Congress that is prevented from being representative both by unequal apportionment and by perverse seniority and other rules, the universities (captive of the destruction and productivity empires), and the military. We wish to illustrate the way in which the pressure of popular demand can become power, by beginning with the success of youth in forcing the government to consider abandoning the draft. This they have done by noncooperation and by outright resistance, but also by a positive and forceful lobbying with their parents and the adult leadership which has brought with it the suasion of a moral stand. The action must continue until the draft is ended for good, and it must continue until the military wing of the violence complex is brought increasingly under control. As this happens, the distinction between military and civilian will be increasingly seen as artificial, and the civilian violence experts will be the next line of attack and subversion. The first step is to press on for a total repeal of conscription as the first and most essential compromise of freedom, and to claim victory for the people when it is ended.

On the basis of that victory, there are other important measures which can be pushed and some steps taken independently, for further control of the violence complex.

These must be done with a clear understanding of the nature of the war machine and how it differs from the traditional military. Chapter 9 has dealt in detail with the garrison society and its implications for control, but it is necessary to be somewhat more specific. The professional military man in uniform is today not a great threat to freedom. As Allen Guttmann recently wrote, "The professional soldier cannot be understood if he is labeled 'authoritarian' and told to stand in a corner." [4] The Department of Defense cannot usefully be described as if it consisted of Prussian militarists. Until recently, professional soldiers often spoke up against foreign military adventures (including the Bay of Pigs).[5] Guttmann continues, "it was the ivy leaguers in the CIA and not the graduates of Annapolis and West Point" who subverted American goals in Cuba at the Bay of Pigs. Vernon Dibble, in his essay "The Garrison Society," makes this point:

> The White House or civilian secretaries censor the speeches of officers or forbid their presentation altogether. But in a garrison society the silencing of men in uniform is irrelevant. For handmaidens of the uniform abound in politics, in scholarship, in the mass media and in business. It makes little difference whether the men who make speeches are generals; or retired generals working for armaments firms; or professors whose research is paid for by the CIA or by the Pentagon; or journalists whose bread and butter depend upon good relationships with Pentagon sources; or Congressmen whose re-election may be jeopardized if the bases in their districts are shut down; or researchers in institutes and think-shops that survive on military contracts; or corporate executives whose firms manufacture missiles or napalm.[6]

The question is therefore not one of civilian control. Civilians in large part now control our military and use it for extraordinarily violent purposes, many of them covert and therefore all the more dangerous to a free society. The Communist Party of the Soviet Union has kept the military under firm civilian control because it has feared a challenge to it from the army. No one would argue, however, that this has meant popular control. The ancients (including Aristotle) often warned against "the men whose only profession is war," and it was the military they feared. Yet there are at least as many civilians as military men today who make their living (and a lucrative one) from war alone. They do not wear uniforms, and their titles and even their specific work may be disarmingly innocuous, but they are paid to produce violence and to see that the violence is marketed at the expense of other priorities. The distinctions between military and civilian are blurred, and popular control is greatly decreased in the process. If we are at all to control the violence complex, we must not trouble ourselves with the threat of mercenaries who may suddenly arise when we start paying the men at the bottom who do the dying and the hand-to-hand killing. We must admit the deep involvement of much of the society in killing by remote control, and we must single out the violence experts for control both of their profession and of their influence in the rest of the society.

Americans still share the view of President Woodrow Wilson that "Americans are the greatest amateurs, the Germans the greatest professionals, and on that basis we will both achieve victory and remain free." The American military is no longer amateur, but rather it is controlled by largely civilian experts of a coolly professional breed. In our day, the military apparatus is supported by professionalism that extends into every part of the American life from real estate to public relations. Secretary McNamara gave a medal in 1965 to the AFL/CIO essentially for propaganda, "for communications media used to promote defense programs." [7] Their contribution was but a small part of the massive publicity network of the violence complex. By 1971, nearly twenty percent of our gross national product, and perhaps twenty percent of our work force, will be dependent on military-related contracts. The armaments industries are no longer content to fill orders devised by Pentagon experts; they now work up their own weapons systems and then sell them to the government. We are no longer able to separate the military and contain it. It has been civilianized, but in the process our society has been militarized.

As Samuel P. Huntington and other experts on civilian-military relations have categorized them, these relationships can be characterized as follows: segregation, subversion, and integration. [8] What is not realized is that any of these can be used by the society to control its military, or by the military to control society. Spain and other military dictatorships illustrate military control of the society by segregation, whereas the United States and England in past decades used segregation to control the military. The Soviet Union has subverted the military to control it, but in the United States, the many former military men now at the top of the so-called "defense" industries have been a subversion of our society by the military-turned-civilians for the purpose of control and wealth. Integration of the military into civilian life began as an effort in this country to control a growing warfare state, but has become itself the process of militarization.

Realizing then the need for popular control over both the civilian and the military wings of the violence complex, it is important that we continue the popular move to end the draft and move as well toward new institutions for the military. In so doing, we may wish to use all three methods of control—subversion, integration, and segregation. The end of the draft will itself provide a helpful segregation in that it will end the myth of a popular amateur military defending the hearth and home of the citizens. The present military is neither amateur nor popular: its ranks are mostly professional, its officer corps is almost entirely professional, and the hidden violence experts at the top are all too professional. The end of the draft will also provide an integration in that the principle of free choice will be reasserted within the military sphere and can lead to other reforms in the military code of justice, so that George Washington's famous phrase can be given meaning: "When we assume the soldier, we do not lay aside the citizen." The draft, as the first act of total control, assumes that the citizen *is* no longer, except as an extension of the will of the state.

NOTES

1. G.W.F. Hegel, *Philosophie der Recht*, Part III, sec. 320–328 (1821).
2. *See* Barrington Moore, Jr., "Revolution in America?" *New York Review of Books*, January 30, 1969. Hannah Arendt, "Reflections on Violence," *New York Review of Books*, February 27, 1969.
3. *Washington Evening Star*, March 11, 1970, p. 6.
4. Allen Guttmann, "Political Ideals and the Military Ethic," *The American Scholar* (Spring 1965), p. 221.
5. Ibid., p. 233.
6. Frank Lindenfeld, ed., *Radical Perspectives on Social Problems* (Los Angeles: California State College, 1968), p. 272.
7. Ibid., p. 276.
8. *See* Samuel P. Huntington, *The Common Defense* (New York: Columbia University Press, 1961); and Harry L. Coles, *Total War and Cold War* (Columbus, Ohio: Ohio State University Press, 1962).

Chapter 11

What the People Can Do

The end of the draft should be viewed as the successful resistance by the people to an unjust law. It would be even more, a successful resistance to an important adjunct of the power of the warfare state. When the draft is ended, however, an army will remain, and it will continue to be the base upon which the violence complex builds. It will be of the utmost importance to exert popular control over the volunteer army and through it over the entire violence complex. There are at least a few of the president's advisors who now argue it will be better for the warfare state to end the irritant of draft resistance, despite the gains which come from the power to draft. These experts doubtless argue that the draft can be reinstituted when "needed." It is therefore necessary for those who have brought an end to the draft to make clear that the state will not again be granted such absolute power over its citizens—that the people are saying "no" to the warfare state in its demand for participation in violent control. The resistance to the draft must be kept up and extended to other underpinnings of the war machine.

The extension of control over the military establishment can be accomplished by two parallel political movements. On the one hand, new institutions should be sought to bring the military out of its privileged haven of secrecy and top priority and into the realm of firm popular control. These may be sought by pressure on members of Congress and by electing Congressmen committed to the changes. The issue of popular control of the military should also be brought into the presidential election and into party politics generally. Where the two traditional parties are resistant to the sweeping suggestions for control, new political coalitions may be built. These coalitions should include as broad a spectrum as possible, and support from all sides in the antidraft movement should provide a basis for them, including the many formerly apolitical groups which were politicized in their work against the draft. Research and symposia at universities and within labor unions, business groups, professional, youth and women's groups might be organized to focus on the need and ways to control the violence complex. Using segregation, integration and subversion of the military establishment, these new institutions will seek to control the military budget, military propaganda, military law, the military aspects of foreign policy, the potential for military rule of the civilian population under the president, and so on. The institutions in every case would involve as many segments of the public as possible and would be free of the traditional executive and other bureaucratic channels of control; that is, they would be *popular* institutions exerting control over both civilian and military wings of the violence complex.

The second movement to parallel the attempt to change

laws and institutions is that of resistance and popular infiltration of existing institutions, or, where the normal channels are unresponsive, the creation of popular parallel institutions. Volunteer soldiers as well as scientists, social scientists, doctors and lawyers, and civilian clerical workers and administrators can be developed as constituencies for popular control and resistance to war-related activities. The various groups within the "peace movement" might develop serious strategies for cultivating constituencies within these groups. For them to do so, they must be willing to leave rhetoric behind them, and in many cases to adapt or desert political or economic doctrines for positive steps toward an awakened America. In each case, the constituency can be developed upon its own self-interest. Volunteer soldiers, for instance, can be made to see that they are citizens first and soldiers second, and that they have undeniable civil rights, unlike the draftee who loses these when he is compelled to enter. Resistance must spread into all parts of the violence complex if popular control is to be successful. Rather than wasting time with theoretical arguments about the possibilities for revolution, the "movement" can begin the task of increasing resistance.

People today have little direct power against the modern state—they cannot possibly smash it. The power of the people is their universal power to say "no." If they will, they can successfully resist any and all institutions of the state by refusing to do its bidding. Such resistance must be well-planned and must involve large numbers of people in a given constituency, but once any one of the key groups is united in resisting the illegitimate authority of the state, it can be successful in curbing its power. The postal strike has shown that some are becoming aware of their ability to act collectively to bargain with the state as well as with business. They are becoming conscious of their power to resist, and of their role in controlling the huge bureaucracy which is the modern state. In order to encourage the rise of this consciousness, peace groups could send their own people into key positions within the various parts of the violence complex, including the volunteer military. Presently this is done only by small socialist groups, often Trotskyite. It could be high on the agenda of every group which challenges the warfare state. Above all, the actions of the peace movement in resisting the state and challenging its war powers must always be calculated to provoke fear in the masters of violence, but never in the people themselves. Especially in America, the witness of the peace movement must be that of many angry but rational and humane individuals of all sorts and from all sectors of the society. Just as no small revolutionary clique can smash the modern state (although it might under some extreme circumstances seize it and rule in terror), neither will such a group capture the imagination or reshape the consciousness of the American people.

Some have charged that a volunteer military will both be more mercenary and difficult to control, and will be made up of the poor and the black. We have already pointed out that the power of the state to confiscate human life is such a threat to freedom that it should be abolished despite side effects. We have also discussed how the real issue of popular control over a civilian-directed violence complex is obscured by talk about controlling mercenary foot-soldiers. It is important to note also that the draftee has not provided "democratization" of the armed forces. Draftees, because they have been forced into service in the first place, are in a poor position to demand their rights or to influence other soldiers to refuse to cooperate in militaristic actions. Those most active in protesting the war in Vietnam have been those least likely to be drafted and even less likely to become front-line "grunts": the college students, most of whom until very recently could prolong deferment into exemption. Inside the army, volunteers have been at least as active as draftees in the antiwar movement. Andy Stapp of the American Servicemen's Union and other GI antiwar leaders have confirmed the fact that many of the soldiers in the "movement" are true volunteers and even second-term enlistees. Recently, I visited GI peace groups at bases in Maryland, North Carolina, Massachusetts, South Carolina, Florida, Kentucky and Tennessee. I found that the new draftee is usually not a prospect for membership in these groups because, as one GI expressed it, he "is scared shitless." *

It is also not true that protest against the war has come largely because of the draft. At no time in Korea or during the slow build-up in Southeast Asia did the draft provoke widespread dissent from those drafted or from their parents, nor did it seem to make Americans more aware of American involvement abroad. Few Americans were at all aware of the steady increase in draft quotas from a monthly four thousand in mid-1964 to over forty thousand in 1966. The Urban Research Corporation of Chicago monitored and summarized the 292 major campus protests during the period January-June 1969. They found that only .03% of these involved protest against the draft.[1] It can hardly be argued that the draft was indirectly responsible for the other protests because of the presence of those on campus who otherwise would not have been students. Anyone familiar

---

* A survey of twenty-five antiwar GIs at Fort Bragg, North Carolina, sponsored by the National Council to Repeal the Draft in March 1970, shows seventeen of them to be volunteer, although some would not have volunteered without the draft. Increase in pay would have provided another incentive for many of these men. Most of the men, sixteen of twenty-five, came from the lower middle class.

with campus protests is aware that both the leaders and the followers come from those groups least likely to be drafted or to serve at the front if drafted, that is, those at the top of their class.

The question of a volunteer military composed mostly of the black and the poor has, as we pointed out above, not troubled the leaders of the black and the poor. They point out, like Congresswoman Shirley Chisholm, that the draft now falls unfairly on poor and black, and that any draft would bring undue burden to poor people who would lose equally with the rich in losing their time and lives, while the wealthy would continue to enjoy profits from the war. The new black consciousness has already made inroads into military recruitment among blacks, as an interoffice memo from the Pentagon pointed out in December 1969. An increase in first-term pay would make military life more appealing to the middle-class and would, if anything, provide a greater economic mix than is now the case with a mixed force of volunteers and draftees. Finally, a change to an all-volunteer system would not alter drastically the present economic and racial balance if only because there are already a majority of volunteers in the system. The problem of an unfair burden on the poor and black is reduced, not increased, by a volunteer system, but it is not ended. The way to attack the problem directly is to attack the racism that is still so basic to our society.

A volunteer military *will* present a problem of control, however, and this question must be dealt with. The voluntary military will be isolated, as is the present force, and perhaps more so. That isolation can be eroded at the bottom and increased at the top—with more civilian values and contacts for the enlisted men, and fewer chances for the officer to use his violence expertise in civilian life (and defense contracts).

We have taken all of these important problems into consideration as we have arrived at some suggestions for a continuation of the antidraft movement beyond ending the draft and into the task of popular control of the violence complex. These suggestions are of the two types mentioned above: new institutions of control, and continued popular resistance; subversion, and parallel institutions. What follow are our suggestions in both of those categories, which are to complement each other.

I. *Institutional Changes to Increase Popular Control of the Violence Complex*[2]

   A. POPULAR CONTROL OF MILITARY AND OTHER VIOLENCE PERSONNEL

      1. The military code should be revised, with final judicial appeal put in the hands of a special Civil Court. Rights of the soldiers to organize unions, to bargain collectively, and to refuse to obey orders in violation of conscience, should be recognized except in time of battle in the battle zones as defined by the commander-in-chief. Such rights presently exist in the Scandinavian countries, Canada, Western Germany, Japan, and elsewhere. Because of American fears of a return to militarism in Germany, the U.S. military provided a military constitution for the West German army which is more liberal than any other in the world. It provides an excellent model for changes here.

      2. At least one-third of the men in every military service at any time should be in their first term. The President's Commission on an All-Volunteer

Armed Force (Gates Commission) has recommended such a high turnover rate, about 75% of the present turnover rate in a mixed draft-volunteer force. At least one-third of the military personnel should be men who intend only one term. These should be solicited through apprenticeship and other training programs.

3. Military officers (including those at the top) should be *obligated* to retire with full pension at age fifty. Former commissioned officers should not be allowed to engage in work connected with the military, except matters related to veterans' benefits. They should be forbidden by law from work with corporations or government agencies which engage in military or intelligence activity or which have more than miminal contracts with the military or intelligence agencies. If necessary, the officers could be retrained at government expense for work in the other fields. Military officers and enlisted men should be allowed full participation in politics, except that those elected to any office should be thereupon discharged from military service.

4. The suggestion of the Gates Commission that the physical and economic isolation of the military be reduced should be taken. Pay-in-kind should be eliminated, since it creates undue dependence upon the military employer. The "PX" and commissary system should be abolished at least in the United States and in developed nations where American troops are stationed. Housing and medical needs should also be civilianized. The chaplaincy should be fully independent, paid by the churches, and made up of civilians. The cor-

ruption and inefficiency in the present military control of all these areas should be added incentive for their civilianization. Fully one-fourth of the present military force should be converted into civilian personnel or eliminated as nonessential. The Gates Commission is known to have intended even stronger recommendations for civilianization, especially of medical facilities, but to have toned these sections down under pressure from the Pentagon.

5. A nonviolent resistance unit should be formed within each branch of the armed forces in which pacifists and others interested in nonviolent defense methods could participate.

B. REDUCTION OF THE POWER OF THE VIOLENCE COMPLEX OVER THE PEOPLE

1. The power of the President as commander-in-chief should be limited (see chapter 7). As his power now stands, he can be dictator if an emergency, in his opinion, requires it. The end of the draft will limit the power of the president to create emergencies abroad or carry on undeclared wars with drafted men. There is further need to prohibit the president from involving American troops abroad except under extraordinary conditions. The war powers of the president should be curtailed by law or perhaps constitutional amendment. A clarification of the meaning of "declaration of war" and the definition of a "state of war" and "national emergency" are also called for.

2. Draft registration and classification must also be abolished, since they are the basis of military

control of civilians, and of state coercion of the people. These may be abolished with no effect on genuine "national security," since such processes could be quickly initiated and computerized if the country were invaded—certainly very unlikely in any case.

3. Article 106 and all other sections of the military code which allow for military control or court martial of civilians should be repealed. This power now allows for the military prosecution of "any person found lurking as a spy about any place, vessel or aircraft" belonging to the military. Since the military owns about 32 million acres of land in the United States and nearly 3 million abroad, and since military hardware is to be found virtually everywhere, these powers are most ominous. The goal here is to segregate military power from the civil society.

4. Either by law or constitutional amendment, it should be made illegal for the armed forces to be used in any way domestically—either to quell rebellions, break strikes or to police troubled areas. State militias should be used sparingly where necessary in these areas, with more emphasis put upon local police locally controlled. This is one of the most pressing aspects of popular control.

C. POPULAR CONTROL OF FOREIGN POLICE AND REDUCTION OF MILITARY INFLUENCE

1. The draft should be viewed as unconstitutional except atfer a formal declaration of war or emergency by Congress, and such declarations should

be limited by constitutional amendment to direct threats of invasion and destruction.

2. The Armed Forces should be reduced as quickly and as greatly as possible, to the level necessary for defense of national borders, but impossible for foreign adventures. Wherever possible, existing security treaty arrangements should be internationalized under the United Nations.

3. The military budget should be greatly reduced, beginning not with manpower, but with missiles and anti-missile systems, and with other weaponry. Ways to increase international control of disarmament should be investigated, with the internationalization or elimination of nuclear weaponry and delivery systems as an ultimate goal. These questions should be taken seriously, with major diplomats and expenditures devoted to them. The existing disarmament agency should be made independent, given a greatly increased budget, and allowed a major public relations campaign at home and abroad. Its director should sit on the National Security Council.

4. There must be a general revamping of U.S. foreign policy. America is a great power and she cannot simply draw back within herself in isolation. Her economic and other powers should be diverted from their present protection of reaction to an aggressive but nonviolent advocacy of social and political change in the direction of democracy, economic justice through redistribution of wealth, and toward internationalization of armaments. Aid of a nonmilitary sort should be increased to those areas where there is economic

backwardness and starvation, but all aid should be multilateral through international agencies, and should be primarily in the form of training, technology, and capital, rather than gifts in kind.

D. GENERAL POPULAR CONTROL OF THE VIOLENCE COMPLEX: ITS BUDGET, POLICIES AND PROPAGANDA

1. An independent, popular control agency should be established over the affairs of the military and civilian violence experts. This agency could be modeled after the Swedish "military ombudsman's office." The ombudsman and his aides are elected by the Parliament. Originally part of the parliamentary ombudsman established in 1809, the military ombudsman has been separate since 1915, although his office is now again connected with the civilian ombudsman. This office provides an independent source of judgment in cases involving military corruption, overstepping the rights of military power and prerogative by officers, and violations of the enlisted men's civil and human rights.* [3]

The American Military Control Agency should be empowered to bring suit in public court in all the matters mentioned above. As in

---

* It is important to note that a military draft continues in Sweden, and that resistance to it continues. The military ombudsman has not been successful because the principle of national security has increasingly overridden that of individual freedom. There is now some evidence that Swedish conscription may be repealed. The presence of American draft resisters has played a role, but a major factor has been the rapid growth of the Swedish Resistance Organization (VCO) which urges resistance against the entire military system.

Sweden, private citizens, military personnel, newspapers, organizations or the control agency itself should be able to initiate investigation. The control agency might be chosen partly by Congress and partly by direct popular vote, or by major popular organizations such as labor unions, the church, women's and youth organizations, and the like. The development of such politically conscious constituencies in America would aid the development of new American publics and the involvement of more Americans in the political process. In any case, the agency should be funded directly by Congress, and its members should be elected for one term only, probably for at least four and not more than six years.

The American military control agency should go beyond its Swedish model. A subdivision of the agency should be created for the study and approval of all military publications, films and other propaganda.

This propaganda and training unit should oversee all military training.

A second military budget unit should be set up to study the military budget with recommendations both to the National Security Council and to the Congress. This unit should have an ample staff of experts to compete with the military in analyzing proposed expenditures.

An intelligence unit should control the CIA and all other military and civilian intelligence agencies, their training and budgets.

An armament industry unit should be set up to oversee all the so-called defense contract arrangements, to make public its findings, and where necessary to bring charges against industries or individuals.

No military officers or former military officers should be allowed to sit on the control agency or work for it. Members of the control agency should not be subject to "security clearance" regulations, but should have full access to all classified data.

The chairman of the military control agency should sit on the National Security Council.

2. As suggested by several bills now before the Congress and by the Congressional Conference on the Military Budget and National Priorities (March 1969), the congressional committees on appropriations and the armed services committees should not be based on seniority and should have rotating membership. No Congressmen with military rank or previous military service (including the reserves) above noncommissioned status should be allowed to serve on these committees.

3. The National Security Council should be enlarged to include all members of the president's cabinet, the chairmen of the appropriate congressional committees, and perhaps two elected members from the national population at large. The power and importance of this council has grown too large for it to be made up solely of the president's military and quasi-military foreign policy advisors.

4. Public hearings on the whole military, CIA and other "security" related budgets should be held with participation of Congressmen and cooperation of the military in all congressional districts.

For the supervision of these hearings, and to supervise work in the field, the military control agency should have an office in each state where there are military bases.

5. The military control agency should study existing secrecy and security clearance regulations, suggesting how these may be reduced to a minimum, or perhaps abolished. Its recommendations should be made public, discussed in hearings in the congressional districts, and voted on by Congress.

II. *Suggestions for Continued Popular Resistance and Parallel Institutions*

The suggested institutional changes just outlined have no political possibility unless a strategy is developed to create public pressure for them. Some such pressure already exists, although it needs a concrete set of goals around which to crystalize. The antidraft movement provides a wide variety of sources for the creation of such continued pressures. Here we present one possible strategy in outline form, based on a belief that the people's chief power in the modern state is its power to resist and ignore the state by creating popular parallel institutions, by subversion, and by saying "no."

A. FORMING AND ENLIGHTENING POPULAR INTERESTS

1. The program and goals of the "movement" must be clarified and concretized. These should be as practical and down-to-earth as possible, and not tied to any doctrinal scheme or to alien, complicated or fear-provoking rhetoric. The institutional changes listed above are possible goals for

the movement in one area, that of popular control of the violence complex.

2. Broad coalitions should be established beyond their present orientation toward public demonstrations. These coalitions should seek to include nonpolitical groups and even conservative political groupings, rather than catering to doctrinally "correct" groups or tiny political sects on the left.

3. The "movement" should bring its message in many forms to as many constituencies as possible on the American scene. Techniques for reaching the American public should be developed and teams established in every community and constituency which are qualified to deal with them on the basis of their particular interests. Such groups should be established near military bases and utilize coffee houses for discussion and organizing. These should be more broadly based·than is the case presently and attempts should be made to involve groups like the YMCA.

4. Writing should be sponsored by as many groups as possible in order to produce a flood of popular books on the control, reduction and eventual elimination of the violence complex. These books should be published by the mass market companies as well as by those catering primarily to universities. A concerted effort should be made to capture several newspapers in the United States, or to buy one major American daily in order to convert it into a national forum for all groups opposing the violence complex.

B. RESISTING THE VIOLENCE COMPLEX

1. Draft resistance of all kinds should be a helpful

base for building resistance to all segments of the violence complex. Resistance by those on the "inside" should especially be fostered, from scientists and university professors to soldiers and clerical workers. It should be limited and clear in its goals (for example: end all remaining chemical-biological war research; or end the security clearance regulations), rational and moderate in its form, but dramatic. The right to strike for federal employees and military could be an issue on which further resistance could be built, and such strikes should be supported and politicized to include antiwar demands where possible. Resistance in the corporations by workers and stockholders should also have top priority. After the draft is over, primary "outsider" resistance should focus on the obstruction of sending American soldiers abroad and on closing down camps where men are trained for "riot" or "special services" duties. In all cases, the resistance should be carefully aimed at the institutions, and not at the soldiers or civilian workers involved.

2. Massive tax refusal on a much wider scale than that of 1970, and planned in advance, should be a major form of resistance. All forms of resistance should be attached to specific goals, such as the creation of the popular institutions for control listed above. Tax refusal might be limited to amounts directly tied to military spending.

C. SUBVERTING THE VIOLENCE COMPLEX

1. Peace organizations and other groups opposed to the violence complex should train and send mem-

bers into all parts of it for the purpose of subverting the values of "security" with the desire for
freedom. This should especially be true in the
military and intelligence organizations. These
people would organize resistance efforts within
the violence complex. They should usually not be
secretive about their feelings, and where possible
should stay within regulations and laws in order
to build as large a base as feasible.

2. The nonviolence unit suggested above, if created,
   would be a useful means of subverting values
   and changing long-held notions about "defense."

D. PARALLEL INSTITUTIONS

1. Where the institutions for controlling and elim-
   inating the violence complex are not created
   officially, they should be created as shadow institutions by the people. An unofficial military control agency, with well-known members perhaps
   elected by unofficial national balloting could be
   a major pressure for the creation of an official
   body.
2. In order to assist resisters to the violence complex, parallel employment agencies, banks, and
   other projects should be set up. These would
   allow the public to refuse to cooperate with war
   projects, either as workers or investors.
3. Where public hearings are not held on the budget
   and other matters connected with the violence
   complex, unofficial hearings should be conducted
   in local areas. Where corruption, crime or militarism is uncovered but goes unchecked, popular
   courts should be assembled to try the individuals
   or corporations involved.

These proposals, both for changes in our laws and institutions, and for action by the people themselves, are an attempt to point the way through and beyond draft repeal to an end to the domination of America by the violence experts. Each of them has in mind above all the need to reassert freedom as a goal beyond the goals of national and economic security. The draft has been one measure among many which have made freedom more distant in our age. Senator Billow of South Dakota said on the Senate floor in 1940 about the draft,

> I regard the vote upon the pending measure to be the most important vote I shall ever be called upon to cast. . . . The question, plainly and bluntly put, is simply this: Shall we abandon the time-honored traditions of a peace-loving, liberty-loving people for that of military despotism? That is the question in a nutshell.[4]

The question today is, can we abandon a course of world domination based on our technological prowess for manipulation and violence? If the people—if the youth—are able to force an end to the draft, there is hope that they will realize their power in time to stop the American violence complex before either tyranny or holocaust is the result.

NOTES

1. Urban Research Corporation, "Student Protests 1969," Chicago, 1970.
2. *Report of the President's Commission on All-Volunteer Armed Force* (Washington, D.C.: U.S. Government Printing Office, 1970), ch. 4, 8, and 12.
3. *See* "The Swedish Parliamentary Ombudsman" (Stockholm: Tryckeribolaget I. Heaggström, 1969); and "The Military Ombudsman in Sweden" (mimeographed report of Embassy of Sweden, 1969).
4. Quoted in *The Draft?*, The American Friends Service Committee (New York City: Hill and Wang, 1968), p. 6.

APPENDIX

Channeling*

One of the major products of the Selective Service classification process is the channeling of manpower into many endeavors, occupations, and activities that are in the national interest. This function is a counterpart and amplification of the System's responsibility to deliver manpower to the armed forces in such a manner as to reduce to a minimum any adverse effect upon the national health, safety, interest, and progress. By identifying and applying this process intelligently, the System is able not only to minimize any adverse effect but to exert an effect beneficial to the national health, safety and interest.

---

* *Channeling* is an official publication of the National Office of the Selective Service System. Originally issued on July 1, 1965, as part of the Selective Service Orientation Kit, the essay was revised and re-issued in September, 1967. The entire Kit is available from the Office of Public Information, Selective Service System, 1724 F Street, N.W., Washington, D.C. 20435. This is the complete text of the 1965 version, Government Printing Office publication number 899. 125.

The line dividing the primary function of armed forces manpower procurement from the process of channeling manpower into civilian support is often finely drawn. The process of channeling by not taking men from certain activities who are otherwise liable for service, or by giving deferment to qualified men in certain occupations, is actual procurement by inducement of manpower for civilian activities which are manifestly in the national interest.

While the best known purpose of Selective Service is to procure manpower for the armed forces, a variety of related processes take place outside delivery of manpower to the active armed forces. Many of these may be put under the heading of "channeling manpower." Many young men would not have pursued a higher education if there had not been a program of student deferment. Many young scientists, engineers, tool and die makers, and other possessors of scarce skills would not remain in their jobs in the defense effort if it were not for a program of occupational deferments. Even though the salary of a teacher has historically been meager, many young men remain in that job, seeking the reward of a deferment. The process of channeling manpower by deferment is entitled to much credit for the large number of graduate students in technical fields and for the fact that there is not a greater shortage of teachers, engineers, and other scientists working in activities which are essential to the national interest.

More than ten years ago, it became evident that something additional had to be done to permit and encourage development of young scientists and trained people in all fields. A million and a half registrants are now deferred as students. One reason the Nation is not in shorter supply of engineers today is that they were among the students deferred by Selective Service in previous years. Similarly, Selective Service student deferments reduced what otherwise would have developed into more serious shortages in teaching, medicine, dentistry, and every field requiring advanced study. The System has also induced needed people to remain in these professions and in industry engaged in defense activities or in the support of national health, safety, or interest.

The opportunity to enhance the national well being by inducing more registrants to participate in fields which relate directly to the national interest came about as a consequence, soon after the close of the Korean episode, of the knowledge within the System that there was enough registrant personnel to allow stringent deferment practices employed during war time to be relaxed or tightened as the situation might require. Circumstances had become favorable to induce registrants, by the attraction of deferment, to matriculate in schools and pursue subjects in which there was beginning to be a national shortage of personnel. These were particularly in the engineering, scientific, and teaching professions.

This was coupled with a growing public recognition that the complexities of future wars would diminish further the distinction between what constitutes military service in uniform and a comparable contribution to the national interest out of uniform. Wars have always been conducted in various ways but appreciation of this fact and its relationship to preparation for war has never been so sharp in the public mind as it is now becoming. The meaning of the word "service," with its former restricted application to the armed forces, is certain to become widened much more in the future. This brings with it the ever increasing problem of how to control effectively the service of individuals who are not in the armed forces.

In the Selective Service System the term "deferment" has been used millions of times to describe the method and means used to attract to the kind of service considered to be most important, the individuals who were not compelled to do it. The club of induction has been used to drive out of areas considered to be less important to the areas of greater importance in which deferments were given, the individuals who did not or could not participate in activities which were considered essential to the defense of the Nation. The Selective Service System anticipates further evolution in this area. It is promoting the process by the granting of deferments in liberal numbers where the national need clearly would benefit.

Soon after Sputnik I was launched it became popular to reappraise critically our educational, scientific, and technological inventory. Many deplored our shortage of scientific and technical personnel, inadequacies of our schools, and shortage of teachers. Since any analysis having any connection with manpower and its relation to the Nation's survival vitally involves the Selective Service System, it is well to point out that for quite some time the System had been following a policy of deferring instructors who were engaged in the teaching of mathematics and physical and biological sciences. It is appropriate also to recall the System's previously invoked practice of deferring students to prepare themselves for work in some essential activity and the established program of deferring engineers, scientists, and other critically skilled persons who were working in essential fields.

The Congress, in enacting the Universal Military Training and Service legislation declared that adequate provisions for national security required maximum effort in the fields of scientific research and development, and the fullest possible utilization of the Nation's technological, scientific, and other critical manpower resources. To give effect to this philosophy, the classifying boards of the Selective Service System defer registrants determined by them to be necessary in the national health, safety, or interest. This is accomplished on the basis of evidence of record in each individual case. No group deferments are permitted. Deferments are granted, however, in a realistic atmosphere so that the fullest effect of channeling will be felt, rather than be terminated by military service at too early a time.

Registrants and their employers are encouraged and required to make available to the classifying authorities detailed evidence as to the occupations and activities in which the registrants are engaged. It is not necessary for any registrant to specifically request deferment, but his selective service file must contain sufficient current evidence on which can be based a proper determination as to whether he should remain where he is or be made available for service. Since occupational deferments are granted for no more than one year at a time, a process of periodically receiving current information and repeated review assures that every deferred registrant continues to contribute to the overall national good. This reminds him of the basis for his deferment. The skills as well as the activities are periodically reevaluated. A critical skill that is not employed in an essential activity does not qualify for deferment.

Patriotism is defined as "devotion to the welfare of one's country." It has been interpreted to mean many different things. Men have always been exhorted to do their duty. But what that duty is depends upon a variety of variables, most important being the nature of the threat to national welfare and the capacity and opportunity

of the individual. Take, for example, the boy who saved the Netherlands by plugging the dike with his finger.

At the time of the American Revolution the patriot was the so-
called "embattled farmer" who joined General Washington to fight
the British. The concept that patriotism is best exemplified by service in uniform has always been under some degree of challenge,
but never to the extent that it is today. In today's complicated warfare when the man in uniform may be suffering far less than the
civilians at home, patriotism must be interpreted far more broadly
than ever before.

This is not a new thought, but it has had new emphasis since the
development of nuclear and rocket warfare. Educators, scientists,
engineers, and their professional organizations, during the last ten
years particularly, have been convincing the American public that
for the mentally qualified man there is a special order of patriotism
other than service in uniform—that for the man having the capacity, dedicated service as a civilian in such fields as engineering, the
sciences, and teaching constitute the ultimate in their expression of
patriotism. A large segment of the American public has been convinced that this is true.

It is in this atmosphere that the young man registers at age 18 and
pressure begins to force his choice. He does not have the inhibitions
that a philosophy of universal service in uniform would engender.
The door is open for him as a student to qualify if capable in a skill
badly needed by his nation. He has many choices and he is prodded
to make a decision.

The psychological effect of this circumstantial climate depends upon
the individual, his sense of good citizenship, his love of country
and its way of life. He can obtain a sense of well being and satisfaction that he is doing as a civilian what will help his country most.
This process encourages him to put forth his best effort and removes
to some degree the stigma that has been attached to being out of
uniform.

In the less patriotic and more selfish individual it engenders a sense
of fear, uncertainty, and dissatisfaction which motivates him, nevertheless, in the same direction. He complains of the uncertainty
which he must endure; he would like to be able to do as he pleases;

he would appreciate a certain future with no prospect of military service or civilian contribution, but he complies with the needs of the national health, safety, or interest—or is denied deferment.

Throughout his career as a student, the pressure—the threat of loss of deferment—continues. It continues with equal intensity after graduation. His local board requires periodic reports to find out what he is up to. He is impelled to pursue his skill rather than embark upon some less important enterprise and is encouraged to apply his skill in an essential activity in the national interest. The loss of deferred status is the consequence for the individual who has acquired the skill and either does not use it or uses it in a nonessential activity.

The psychology of granting wide choice under pressure to take action is the American or indirect way of achieving what is done by direction in foreign countries where choice is not permitted. Here, choice is limited but not denied, and it is fundamental that an individual generally applies himself better to something he has decided to do rather than something he has been told to do.

The effects of channeling are manifested among student physicians. They are deferred to complete their education through school and internship. This permits them to serve in the armed forces in their skills rather than in an unskilled capacity as enlisted men.

The device of pressurized guidance, or channeling, is employed on Standby Reservists of which more than 2½ million have been referred by all services for availability determinations. The appeal to the Reservist who knows he is subject to recall to active duty unless he is determined to be unavailable is virtually identical to that extended to other registrants.

The psychological impact of being rejected for service in uniform is severe. The earlier this occurs in a young man's life, the sooner the beneficial effects of pressured motivation by the Selective Service System are lost. He is labeled unwanted. His patriotism is not desired. Once the label of "rejectee" is upon him all efforts at guidance by persuasion are futile. If he attempts to enlist at 17 or 18 and is rejected, then he receives virtually none of the impulsion the System is capable of giving him. If he makes no effort to enlist and as a result is not rejected until delivered for examination by the

Selective Service System at about age 23, he has felt some of the pressure but thereafter is a free agent.

This contributed to establishment of a new classification of I-Y (registrant qualified for military service only in time of war or national emergency). That classification reminds the registrant of his ultimate qualification to serve and preserves some of the benefit of what we call channeling. Without it or any other similar method of categorizing men in degrees of acceptability, men rejected for military service would be left with the understanding that they are unfit to defend their country, even in war time.

An unprejudiced choice between alternative routes in civilian skills can be offered only by an agency which is not a user of manpower and is, therefore, not a competitor. In the absence of such an agency, bright young men would be importuned with bounties and pirated like potential college football players until eventually a system of arbitration would have to be established.

From the individual's viewpoint, he is standing in a room which has been made uncomfortably warm. Several doors are open, but they all lead to various forms of recognized, patriotic service to the Nation. Some accept the alternatives gladly—some with reluctance. The consequence is approximately the same.

The so-called Doctor Draft was set up during the Korean episode to insure sufficient physicians, dentists, and veterinarians in the armed forces as officers. The objective of that law was to exert sufficient pressure to furnish an incentive for application for commission. However, the indirect effect was to induce many physicians, dentists, and veterinarians to specialize in areas of medical personnel shortages and to seek outlets for their skills in areas of greatest demand and national need rather than of greatest financial return.

Selective Service processes do not compel people by edict as in foreign systems to enter pursuits having to do with essentiality and progress. They go because they know that by going they will be deferred.

The application of direct methods to effect the policy of every man doing his duty in support of national interest involves considerably more capacity than the current use of indirection as a method of allocation of personnel. The problem, however, of what is every man's duty when each individual case is approached is not simple. The question of whether he can do one duty better than another is a problem of considerable proportions and the complications of logistics in attempting to control parts of an operation without controlling all of it (in other words, to control allocation of personnel without controlling where people eat, where they live, and how they are to be transported) adds to the administrative difficulties of direct administration. The organization necessary to make the decisions, even poor decisions, would, of necessity, extract a large segment of population from productive work. If the members of the organization are conceived to be reasonably qualified to exercise judgment and control over skilled personnel, the impact of their withdrawal from war production work would be severe. The number of decisions would extend into billions.

A quarter billion classification actions were needed in World War II for the comparatively limited function of the Selective Service System at that time. Deciding what people should do, rather than letting them do something of national importance of their own choosing, introduces many problems that are at least partially avoided when indirect methods, the kind currently invoked by the Selective Service System, are used.

Delivery of manpower for induction, the process of providing a few thousand men with transportation to a reception center, is not much of an administrative or financial challenge. It is in dealing with the other millions of registrants that the System is heavily occupied, developing more effective human beings in the national interest. If there is to be any survival after disaster, it will take people, and not machines, to restore the Nation.

July 1, 1965

About the Authors

THOMAS REEVES is the National Director in Washington of the National Council to Repeal the Draft, a coalition of representatives from fifty organizations ranging from the Resistance to the YMCA, the Catholic Peace Fellowship and the ADA. He is Associate Professor of Political Science at the Federal City College in Washington.

Born in Nashville, Tennessee, in 1939, Mr. Reeves received the B.A. degree from Birmingham-Southern College, the M.A. degree from American University School of International Service, the STB degree from Harvard University, and the D.Phil. degree from Humbolt University, Berlin, Germany. He also studied at the Otto-Suhr Institute and the Free University in West Berlin.

He was ordained a Methodist pastor and served parishes in Alabama and Massachusetts. He has taught at Schiller College in West Germany, and the American University in Washington. He has published articles in *The Christian Century, The Nation, Religious Education, The Washington Free Press,* and *Der Politologe* (West Berlin).

KARL HESS is a sponsor of the National Council to Repeal the Draft, and is a contributing editor to *Ramparts* and a visiting fellow at the Institute for Policy Studies. Born in Washington, D.C., in 1923, Mr. Hess has worked as a radio news commentator, a newspaper reporter, and an editor. He was special consultant to President Eisenhower on foreign affairs, was one of the writers of the 1960 Republican Platform, and was, from 1963 until 1965, principal speechwriter for Senator Barry Goldwater. Mr. Hess has, as well, worked and written for such conservative institutes as the Institute for Strategic Studies at Georgetown University and the Hoover Institution on War, Revolution, and Peace at Stanford University. His political views began to change in 1967 because of his judgment about the Vietnam war.